To my parents Jude and Chris, for the fantastical
hand-painted bedroom that kicked this all off,
and to Ollie, for being the most colourful part of my life.

KALEIDOSCOPE

Modern Homes in Every Colour

Amy Moorea Wong

Hardie Grant

BOOKS

CONTENTS

INTRODUCTION

Ask most people what their favourite colour is and you're likely to get replies that roam the rainbow, but walk into their homes and it'll probably be a different story. When discussing the idea of the home and colour, the word 'fear' crops up surprisingly often – it turns out many of us are genuinely scared of mixing the two. Is it that we're afraid we'll choose tones we'll later go on to dislike? That our choices will be deemed strange or wrong? That the scheme will quickly turn into an embarrassing, forgotten trend?

Kaleidoscope challenges this notion. This book is a glorious gallery of homes by celebrated global designers and creatives spanning properties doused in rich pigment to those brought to life by smaller bursts of colour, and everything in between. It's full of knowledge, advice and encouragement on how to confidently make a space brighter, fill it with your personality and add a dash of intrigue.

These homes are real, lived-in spaces, put together not for photography, but to travel through daily life in and to make those within them feel good. Each is an elegant exploration of how to use colour in a sophisticated, timeless, grown-up yet playful way. They are experiments in colour that surprise and inspire.

I thought I knew what a colourful home looked like, but I have come to realise that everyone's idea of 'colourful' is wildly different. To some, it means vividity, a slap in the face, wow-that's-bold level of deep saturation, primary-style shades drawn straight from a box of Lego or a set of crayons. To others, it's more delicate – pastel colours infused with white, 'muddied' tones tinged with grey or rich, intense hues touched by black. What we are not talking about here are rooms that are dedicated to white, grey or black, and certainly not about spaces immersed in beige, magnolia, ivory or any other of their bland pals.

There seems to be a general consensus that it takes bravery to buy a colourful artwork, or cushion, or chair, or shade of paint, which is a rather bizarre concept when you step back and consider it. To echo what the brilliant people in this book say over and over again: what's the worst that can happen? You can reupholster that mustard chair, eBay that multicoloured collection of cushions and paint over that blush door. You can even change those mint tiles and swap out those emerald curtains, which is more time- and money-consuming of course, but very doable. The overriding opinion of the experts in these pages is that the beautiful, soul-enriching end result is worth the risk.

What has become very clear to me is that colour in the home – however you define it – more often than not equals happiness, joy and optimism. It has the power to lift you up and make walking through the door a highlight of the day. It's a powerful, useful tool, able to put a smile on

your face and a spring in your step, and, like any other tool, there are techniques to harness it so it works properly. Step by step, nice and easy. Building your palette can be guided by anything, from noting the colours of your favourite restaurant to the activities you enjoy or from what you're wearing, by looking at the shades you already live with, be they on objects, clothing or make-up, by pulling natural tones from the sky, the forest or the sea, or by throwing caution to the wind and going with your instinct – rules be damned.

For me, interiors have always been about self-expression and creativity – the place where we live offering a blank canvas, a chance to do something interesting and reflect who we are. It's exciting. It's an opportunity. When surrounded by a space you have grown used to or a 360-degree view of whites, greys and neutrals, of course the idea of clicking 'confirm' on that indigo sofa or opening a can of lilac emulsion seems like a leap into the unknown. But trust me. Trust us – from Dublin interior-design house Kingston Lafferty Design, which creates dreamlike universes with its enchanting palette, to Perth design studio State of Kin with its nature-meets-brightness approach, San Francisco interior-design firm Regan Baker Design's calming yet exciting hues, and the rest of these contemporary, chic, creative designers – the call is always the same: Do it. Do it. Do it.

STINE

GOYA

For Stine Goya, founder and creative director of the eponymous Copenhagen-based fashion label, home is a peaceful bubble. While her job involves concocting runway-ready collections of clothing renowned for their dazzling palette, expressive prints, daring silhouettes and playful attitude, at home things are – a little – more serene. 'For me, interior design represents unlimited creativity, I approach it playfully and endlessly experiment, drawing inspiration from colours, shapes, textures, objects, art ...' she explains. 'It's quite different from designing fashion. Designing my own home was purely something I did for pleasure.'

Known for breaking boundaries and flouting the rules – there is no neutral Scandi minimalism at the House of Goya – Stine's home is adventurous but simultaneously soft and soothing, brightness converging with the not-very-bright and meeting in the middle. It somehow combines excitement and enchantment with an alluring sense of the easy-going. 'I wanted an intimate yet creative universe as soon as you enter the house,' she says. 'While it's colourful, I created spaces that have calm vibes, otherwise my eyes would start to complain.'

'I like crafting little "wow" moments that make the house unique and personal, spots that capture the essence of the interior and make you happy every time you're there,' Stine explains. These instants of exclamation can range from pleasing combinations of colour, pattern and texture, such as the placement of a simple square cushion alongside a patterned round design (hello downstairs seating area), to the curated collection of curious three-dimensional objects dotted throughout (spot the blue wooden rocking horse).

While visually it's hard to define a thread to the home, or link between some of the rooms, it all somehow glides together and works as a whole, while individual areas are given space to shine. 'Each room has a different mood and multiple styles are mixed together to create a new, personal aesthetic,' says Stine. 'It doesn't follow trends and is more of a collection of memories and moments – I really love it when interiors tell a story about the people living in it and creating it. It shouldn't feel like a showroom.'

'A home has to have character and personality; if it's too anonymous or stereotypical, it can become quite boring,' Stine says. 'It also depends so much on location – being in the centre of a vibrant city such as Copenhagen, where we are, almost calls for a colourful, artistic and lively flair.' There's no danger of a tedious time here. When crossing the threshold, you are immediately encased in a fresh lilac, overlooked by hovering pendant lamps lighting the way in coordinating candy colours. 'The lilac sets the mood when you enter the house,' she continues. 'It's eye-catching and makes opening the front door a pleasant, soothing experience. The colour immediately drags you in and invites you to discover more.'

Previous page. File Under Pop's 'True Blue' paint turns the ceiling in the hallway and the house's subsequent two floors into an exaggerated skyscape. 'Hallways and staircases are the perfect rooms to experiment in and be creative with,' says Stine. 'The darker blue on the ceiling closes the space and develops this kind of cocoon, whereas the lighter colour contrasts and opens it up.'

Left. The entrance becomes a pastel-hued portal painted all over in 'Purple Fame' by File Under Pop. The pale floating orbs of Helle Mardahl's 'Bon Bon' pendant lamps further reinforce the house's palette.

Venture further into the home and there's a cheerful blue ceiling waiting to keep you on your toes – sky blue this is not – followed by a kitchen permanently basking in a golden, butterscotch-y sunlight. The gentility of the pale-lemon downstairs living room is decisively interrupted by fizzing aqua upholstery, the bedroom's peach backdrop plays host to an assortment of singing shades, textures and shapes, while the dressing room places blocks of gentle cornflower blue and peach next to pillar-box red, pea green and rich burgundy as if it were the easiest thing in the world.

'It's is actually quite a long process deciding on colours and how to put them together,' explains Stine. 'It always starts with assessing the light, which is very important for making decisions. It's really is a process of trial and error; you can find the perfect shade but once in a space it can change so much. When creating a room, I like to put together all of the colours that have to co-exist – the paint, carpet, furniture, curtains, etc – to view them as one story. Only then can I start working on combinations and try out different options to create the spectrum I want to see and feel.'

The pastel palette in the home isn't the faded, ice-cream, delicate tones you might expect. Stine shows us how to go bold with pale shades. It's what she pairs them with that brings out their energy as well as making the most of their muted mood. 'Pastels are a great way to start using colours in interiors as they're often very soothing and have a calmness to them,' the designer explains. 'Since they all have white undertones they are pretty easy to blend – I love to use pastels as a background palette and mix in details in deeper and more intense colours to create a contrast and to make them pop even more.'

'A life filled with colour brings a daily dose of happiness,' says Stine. 'Interior design is very personal – that's its overall purpose: to make spaces meaningful so you feel good in them. Start by adding small, colourful details and take it from there. I can guarantee that you won't be bored and that it will reveal a new perspective on your style.'

Left. An intricate painting by John Kørner adds a bolt of brightness and is contrasted by the simplicity of Muller Van Severen's 'Duo Seat'.

Opposite. A playful mix of colours and materials comes together in the downstairs seating area, overlooked by an artwork by Tal R. 'Working on the palette was like putting together a puzzle,' says Stine. 'I fell in love with the custom-made aqua couch and went from there. It's a very fun and unexpected combination which is both exciting and harmonious.'

In contrast to the surrounding spaces, the living room is pared back colour-wise, which introduces visual room for interesting objects. 'Finding the right balance in your house is extremely important,' says Stine. 'Sometimes you need some neutral areas for the more colourful rooms to be able to stand out, to give the statement furniture and art pieces in the living room space to breathe.'

The kitchen is doused in the warm tones
of a never-ending soft sunset thanks to
Le Corbusier colour '32001 Blanc' paint
covering the walls and its hearty timber tones.
'The walls are a soft and especially calming
colour that almost gives off light and radiates
within the space, which we needed because
in dark winter times it gets limited daylight,'
explains Stine.

Awash with soft 'Calamine' by Farrow & Ball,
the shade of the bedroom is a colourful
cave. 'It's a very dreamy colour and just feels
cosy,' says Stine. 'It gives an extremely soft
glow when the light hits it, which is the best
atmosphere to wake up to.'

Do you have a favourite colour for the home?

'Purple Fame' from File Under Pop. It's an extremely soothing colour and, while quite prominent, it is also light and neutral at the same time which makes it very easy to combine with other colours.

Are any hues banned from the house?

I wouldn't use pure primary colours in my home or fashion collections, apart from for very specific purposes, as they can easily become too dominant.

What's the easiest/cheapest/ quickest way to add colour to a home?

Definitely by painting or adding curtains.

How do you approach accessorising colourfully?

Go more for tone on tone than only working with strong contrasts – it's the combination of both that results in the most beautiful spaces.

Where would you add a surprise hit of colour?

Hanging a painting on a coloured wall which accentuates accents in the piece makes it stand out even more – art pieces can really benefit from colour, it creates much more impact than white.

Have you had any decorating disasters?

Yes, of course – it often happens when I have too little time to consider my colour choices. It's the process of experimenting that leads you to the best colour mixes in the end.

Where do you visit for colour inspiration?

An old monastery in Puglia called Il Convento Santa Maria di Constantinopoli. It's an amazing bed-and-breakfast that always inspires me. It's pure joy to go there and soak in the colourful world they create.

Who are you following for interiors inspiration?

Magazines such as Sight Unseen (@_sightunseen_) and Dezeen (@dezeen) for a daily dose of inspiration, not only for colours but also for young and upcoming architects, designers and artists.

Top tips for decorating with colour

1. Remember that your home is not a showroom.
2. Don't be afraid to try things out. Trial and error is key.
3. Colour can be found in many different ways by combining art, materials, textures …
4. Remind yourself it is a curated space – more isn't always more.
5. Try to create a universe that makes you feel good.

The 'Match' wardrobe by Muller Van Severen for Reform makes a statement in the dressing room with its customisable combination of bright and pastel shades. 'It gives me energy, which is perfect when you get dressed in the morning,' says Stine.

EARL

OF EAST

For Niko Dafkos and Paul Firmin, co-founders of independent lifestyle brand Earl of East, home is a place to experiment in, an evolving aesthetic that doesn't stand still for too long, and which doubles as a location for photographing soon-to-be-sold design objects. Their house in – yes – East London is a reflection of their work environment, and vice versa. To some this would be less than ideal, but not so with this curated approach which combines an ever-changing, subtle, drawn-from-nature base with small moments of discovery. A feeling of warmth – and that you are very welcome – pervades the home (and the stores). The palette is soothing and approachable, at times like being engulfed in a friendly hug, elsewhere letting you browse undisturbed. 'Imagine the house is shoppable and it's easy to see the link to the stores, aesthetically they blend into each other,' the pair say. 'We wanted to create a space that's full of colour in a city that isn't.'

Although it's now infused with life, unobtrusive pigment and a calm, sanctuary-like feel, when Niko and Paul moved in, it was quite the opposite – a box-fresh, brilliant white-soaked new build. The couple took time to live in the house before jumping to decorating, observing where the light moved and how they used the spaces, so when it came to picking up a paint brush they were armed with an intimate knowledge of every room.

Spending their daylight hours in the sun-filled kitchen and dining room, they embraced the living room for its more enveloping qualities, steeped in a rich ochre, coordinating with the sofa tone-on-tone style. 'We realised quite quickly that the living room was never going to be great at any time of the day, so there was no point trying to play with it,' they explain. 'It barely gets any natural light so we decided to make it even darker.' The study was lifted with a sunny sky blue, the bedroom colour-blocked in tonal shades, the guest room ruled over by bright textiles, and the kitchen and dining room given over to a muddy, neutral greenish yellow which changes so much with the light it's hard to believe the two areas share a paint can.

Overall, the palette is garden-derived, heavily pigmented yet pared back. 'We want the colours to be a statement, but not overly loud or challenging – dynamic but never too in your face,' Niko and Paul explain. 'The thread that runs throughout is a natural take on colourful shades that work together to emit a calmness, so the home becomes a sanctuary.' The thread is also rather a literal one, the palette of sandy shades, blues and hints of burgundy inspired, unsurprisingly, by the shop, more specifically by the 'Shay' blanket by Ferm Living, which first lent it its tonal hues to the main bedroom (where it still lives) before spreading through the entire house.

This is by no means the home's first iteration, and it certainly won't be its last. 'It feels like it's ever-evolving,

The living room is a den of 360-degrees of ochre, painted in 'Muga' by Paint & Paper Library, with Niko and Paul accepting the room's lack of natural light and harnessing it. 'You feel like you're in a warm cave,' they say. 'It's both overpowering and cosy.' A vivid yellow artwork by Studio Lenca adds a blaze of the unexpected: 'It shouldn't work in principle, yet it complements the walls so well,' explain the pair.

so whenever the time is right – and the budget is available – we refresh a room and move it on to the next phase,' Niko and Paul explain. 'We started off very grey and dark and then, over time, we introduced more colour, texture and depth.' Once the greyscale was banished, barely a hint of black or white was left behind in a house now dedicated to peaceful natural shades and artful pops of brightness. 'The grey was a bit dark and oppressive,' they say. 'Now, you're happy to walk into the ochre cocoon of the living room and see a flash of blue from the study. The new colours have definitely made us enjoy the space more – they're uplifting.'

While each room has a very clear colour personality and dedicated shade, hues from other spaces bleed into one another, creating an overall palette where the focus fluctuates from room to room. There's only one strict rule – ceilings must get involved. 'We love decking a whole room out in a colour,' Paul and Niko explain. 'A white ceiling is harsh and divides the space – when you step into a room that's fully painted it feels bigger. In some ways including the ceiling in the room's palette is less bold than leaving it white, even though it feels like a big step.'

For Paul and Niko, colour is to be tested and explored, creating moments of contentment before transforming into something fresh. 'Try it,' they suggest. 'It can be as simple as adding textiles, which are really easy to change. When people say they're afraid of using colour, often it's knowing how to put shades together – start with one or two tones that you like and they can become a common link through the home. You can be big and bold, but there are ways to add colour to a house without it being too over the top.'

Opposite. The dining room's neutral, natural sandy painted backdrop of 'String' by Farrow & Ball is unfixed, changing its hue depending on the time of day and the light. 'Sometimes it seems yellow and at other times a bit greener,' the couple explain. 'It plays with the daylight and is different depending on the season. It's warm, but it can also be bright.'

In the kitchen, small accessories add hints of colour, creating points of interest, and tie in with the overall scheme. The inherited pistachio-toned cabinets chime with the sandy walls, allowing small blocks of colour to draw the eye on a calming backdrop.

Above. While it may have white surfaces, Niko and Paul see the guest bedroom as 'the most intense and colourful room in the house', as smaller pieces bring in the brightness. 'It is colourful, but it's done in a democratic way,' they explain. 'The colourful pieces are really easy to change and update.'

Opposite. The deep navy 'Scotch Blue' paint by Farrow & Ball seemed like a colourful alternative for the previously grey bedroom, which is where the refined palette started; 'We took the opportunity to do something bolder on the wall behind the bed,' the pair explain. A thread of navy runs through the home via objects and art, drawing individual rooms, and the house overall, together.

Do you have a favourite colour for the home?

We always look at Farrow & Ball. The paint is always really consistent and there's always a great narrative behind the colours – they always feel like they stand the test of time.

What's the best way to bring colour inside?

Textiles. They're a really quick, easy, affordable way to change the interior space. We have more cushions on the bed than we'll ever need.

Are any hues banned from the house?

While we have small elements of burgundy in the house, we're not a big fan of reds – they're a bit aggressive – so we don't foresee a red room or a terracotta room.

How do you approach accessorising colourfully?

Use groupings – threes. Have a trio (or other odd number) of objects and create landscapes with taller and shorter heights. It just looks more interesting that way.

Where would you add a surprise hit of colour?

It's artwork in our house. We have pieces in interesting places all over the house – behind doors, at the top of the stairs, leaning against walls …

Have you had any decorating disasters?

We're ready for a change from the ochre, but it's definitely not a disaster!

How would you name your own paint range?

Our scent collection is named by location with words that are commonly used in that place, for example 'Greenhouse' is a vine-tomato fragrance. We would use something that resonates before you have to explain it.

Where do you visit for colour inspiration?

We love going to independent stores when we travel, and we always really like to go into the Barbican, into the conservatory for a hit of green.

Top tips for decorating with colour

1. If you are going to go bold with colour, always include the woodwork and the ceiling, because it makes the space feel complete and a lot bigger.

2. Use colourful textiles as a way to lift or change a space affordably and with minimal effort.

3. Green life – plants and the odd bright bunch of flowers are really great for the mood, as well as just for making the space feel a lot cosier.

4. Play with what you've got – it looks really weird when people try to turn a space into something it isn't.

5. Link a scent to a colourful space to create an aesthetic for all of the senses; it's all about environments being multi-sensory.

Drenched in Dulux's 'First Dawn', the office walls become a gloriously cloudless painted sky, and a punch of brightness in the home that is glimpsed every time the stairs are climbed. 'The room was very, very bright, small with a big window, so we played with that and added a bit of fun,' say Niko and Paul.

REGAN

BAKER

It started with a tin of canary yellow paint. For this compact San Francisco home, the brief was 'bring in colour', and interior designer Regan Baker, founder of eponymous firm Regan Baker Design, didn't waste any time fulfilling it. After a simple, yet courageous makeover, a standard not-very-friendly steel staircase, which weighed heavily on the living room, was transformed into something akin to a fairground ride. Now, the swirling sculptural twist of lemon sets the tone for the home, creating a powerful first impression for the cheerful-yet-calm interior, as well as an unforgettable way to transition between upstairs and down.

Considered colour is Regan's calling card, tones that dally between the natural – a lot of timber to back up the indoor–outdoor feel of the gentle blues and greens she is drawn to – and the extravagant, which are often taken from a peek into her client's closets. 'I'm ever-inspired by nature. It's calming and inviting, as well as a good base for additional shades,' Regan explains. 'Fashion is also a starting point for me. I like to ask clients if I can take a picture of what's in their wardrobes, as that says a lot about who they are and how much colour and pattern resonates with them'.

The tones here are an understated balance of peaceful pastels and wow-factor brights, living somewhat surprisingly in harmony. While the explosion of yellow initially entertains the eye, there's a tranquil undercurrent in the softness in the timber, the outdoorsy sky and plant hues and the light-capturing white walls (so all-encompassing yet so easily unnoticed) that permeate the home. 'A pop of colour within a more neutral palette allows that bold brilliance to really fizz, while the calming, more grounded environment around it means the eye isn't overwhelmed,' explains Regan. 'It creates an amazing contrast, and feels like happiness shining through'.

While Regan's approach to building a palette bounces off nature, the contents of wardrobes and also her client's existing pieces (namely art), she also incorporates a tone-on-tone rule to govern her approach to interiors colouring. 'It's an important trick to guide you and keep the room from becoming too overwhelming,' she says. 'It's a reminder to repeat a colour, or a shade of a colour, throughout a room, or to help maintain balance in a cohesive, soothing and cheerful way.' Thus, the gleeful yellow of the stairs also finds itself in the vivid living room artwork by Jenny Sharaf (which was commissioned to incorporate the exact hues found throughout the space) and on smaller accessories, while various versions of blue dance around the entire home, inconspicuously pulling it all together.

Bleached walls may take up a high percentage of the home's decoration, but there's no chance of coming away without tonal rainbows in your eyes. 'If you want bright and light, white's a great shade to start with. It gives colour

The star of the house, the sculptural yellow stairs (previous page), set a lively tone, painted in tactile matte Benjamin Moore 'Lemon Grove' (with a protective clear layer on the treads). 'The stairs are such an interesting focal point, they really add narrative to the room – the yellow is so fun, a real mood brightener,' describes Regan. 'I really think if you are open to embracing colour then it's go hard or go home. I do not think this house would be the same without the yellow staircase.'

Eye-popping colours are grounded with natural materials such as the stone fire surround, the travertine-topped table and woven organic elements, as well as lashings of white in the living room, creating depth and texture as well as excitement. The palette is pulled together by the bespoke Jenny Sharaf artwork above the fireplace.

room to breathe – make sure you have a lot of it!' Regan advises. 'Then think about wood and natural materials to bring in warmth, and then consider art, fabric and rugs which can be a jumping-off point for the overall palette – it'll soon take on a life of its own.' Her advice for the more pigment-hesitant among us? 'When in doubt, paint it out! You can always go back and redo it a different colour – just do it, go big' she smiles, 'Paint is such an easy starting point and a great way to say who you are without having to break the bank. Or choose a piece of art and mix in accessories that match it. Don't forget to play with variations of the same colour to make it all less scary.'

In this house, colour spells joy, dispatched thoughtfully and deliberately yet with a happy-go-lucky sense of the fanciful. 'Colour is such a huge part of how a room or a home feels and it really represents your personality,' says Regan. 'Would I say if you have a colourless home, you're a little less interesting? Maybe.'

Left. A space for the eye to rest, the small kitchen was left a crisp white to counteract the spectrum of colours in the living room.

Opposite. Intense artworks and splashes of black strike a darker tone in the dining area. 'We worked around the client's existing art and balanced it with zesty pastel shades, as well as serious deeper tones which dramatically juxtapose the home's overall lighthearted mood,' Regan explains.

The vivid tones of the artwork are reflected in the upholstery in the office, which, like the rest of the home, relies on a bright base of white to support rich doses of colour.

42

The bedroom's pretty palette stemmed from the fantastical curtains by Josef Frank at Svenskt Tenn, which make an electric impact on the room, Regan layering – mostly – the more subdued pastel shades from the pattern to keep the space soothing for sleep. 'The curtain needed to make a statement when you walk into the room – if you want to make an impact with a design or object, it should be the first thing you see when you enter,' explains Regan. 'It sets the tone, personalising the space, and is a striking conversation piece.'

The architectural checked tiles are garnished
with mint without fully committing to it,
maintaining a clean feeling in the bathroom while
simultaneously adding a touch of playfulness.

Demonstrating Regan's tone-on-tone approach, the bathroom is a compilation of different shades of green.

Which colours do you like to combine?

Any colour paired with wood tones or nudes is a 'go to'. I tend to gravitate towards blues and greens because they remind me of nature and create a soothing, cheerful feel.

Are any hues banned from the house?

I have no colour bias! That said, I do avoid colour pairings that are too holiday-specific or thematic. No themed rooms, please!

Which space most benefits from colour?

Anywhere you'd like to make a statement – think staircases (of course!), fireplaces, decorative woodwork or a furniture piece.

What's the easiest/cheapest/quickest way to add colour to a home?

Throw blankets and cushions!

Have you had any decorating disasters?

Early in my career, I chose a white paint that was so, so wrong. The green-tinted glass in the windows turned it a minty yellow-green. It was terrible. I learned a valuable lesson in the importance of testing paint on multiple walls in different lights!

How would you name your own paint range?

I'd skew towards names with a story behind them and/or that have a connection with nature. For example, another option for the yellow in this project could be 'Meyer Yellow', a nod to the Meyer lemons growing in our back yard.

Top tips for decorating with colour

1. Don't be afraid to be bold in your colour selection. It's your home!

2. Take a peek in your own wardrobe to get a feel for colours you gravitate towards.

3. Make pops of colour sophisticated by incorporating subtle textures and organic elements.

4. Remember the negative space when using colour. Allow a black or white place for your eye to rest.

5. Don't forget the small details which say 'Hello, I love colour!' in an unexpected way.

EVA-MARIE

EWILKEN

Built in 1919 and filled with furniture and design objects in an array of styles, ages and colours, it's hard to tell which era the Copenhagen apartment of stylist Eva-Marie Wilken exists in. Ornate ceilings, original tiles, handmade terrazzo and elegant proportions point to a time gone by, and classic mid-century furniture pieces edge us closer to the present, while a spritely pastel palette updates the look by a further few decades. Add in abstract art, expressive wallpaper and sculptural lighting and the final feeling is very much up to date – contemporary with a side order of richness and history. 'I am drawn to colours that look like they have been in use for many years, and that could have been in the apartment centuries ago,' Eva-Marie says. 'My home is created without a link to a particular time or trend and I like to mix pieces that do not necessarily fit together – I want to retain an authentic atmosphere, but also make function and delightfulness top priorities.'

The walls' sugared-almond palette of delicate pinks and blues supports and adds to the wedding-cake aesthetic of the decorative plasterwork ceilings, creating a charismatic juxtaposition of old and new. For Eva-Marie, the scheme's jumping-off point was a much-loved piece of seating to which her signature pale blue paint was matched. 'The blue walls came from the shade of my 40-year-old sofa,' she explains. 'The colour has followed me for years – it's a colour my mother used – I've painted all sorts of spaces with it, I will never get tired of it. Adding pink to the blue creates a bit of excitement and contrast, and makes the apartment less predictable.'

For somewhere now so inherently colourful, the space is surprisingly dependent on white, from the blanched ceilings, tiles and painted woodwork left behind 100 years ago, to the white-based pastels that cover almost every wall. What draws Eva-Marie to such subdued hues is the atmosphere they create and the feeling they infuse her home with. 'Pastels create a gentle mood,' she says. 'I find colours with a lot of white much less invasive than bolder tones.'

The simple, soothing shades are lifted and enlivened with flashes of black in almost every room, which anchor the delicate colours and remind us that we are not, in fact, in a spun-sugar castle. The dark elements – often employed with linearity or in small doses – give the pastels an edge, heightening their pigments by contrast and adding depth and physical hardness to the soft tints. 'Black accents make the apartment less sweet and add a small element of surprise,' says Eva-Marie.

The most unexpected element in the apartment is the wallpaper, often unobtrusively folded into the home as a feature wall, backing up a set of coordinating curtains or sitting quietly atop a tiled portion of wall, subtly chiming

Pale blue walls painted in '4472' by Flügger encircle the living room, challenging the period details with its sugary palette. 'I thoroughly enjoy the way old and new come together in the apartment, it's wonderful to think of how life here once was,' says Eva-Marie.

with the home's pink-and-blue-ness but with more oomph. Almost every space is impacted by a decorative paper, either as a standalone wall or bought into a space as a view through a door frame, introducing a slice of pattern and manipulating scale. An oversized palm-leaf motif in the workroom adds to the pretty dolls' house feel, whereas the navy Art Deco florals in the dining area both contrast and complement the sky-blue walls that surround it. 'The darker blue wallpaper is the only design in the apartment that differs from the calm pastel palette,' says Eva-Maria. 'It forms a frame around the room, as well as creating a focal point.'

With its pretty powdery palette, this apartment so easily could have developed a baby-ish quality, and yet some cleverly deployed accents, shades and patterns have kept it firmly in the sophisticated sphere. It's a lesson in being true to the tones that speak to you and which make you feel good. Because what else matters? 'Emotionally, these are colours that make me safe and happy,' says Eva-Marie. 'For me, strong colours sap all of the energy — my light, gentle tones are never demanding or intrusive. I use what I find beautiful.'

Opposite. The blocky black dining table becomes light and airy surrounded in and reflecting the pale blue walls painted in '4472' by Flügger.

Above left. Eva-Marie's multifunctional studio/office/workshop is presided over by the retro fronds of Cole & Son's 'Palm Leaves' wallpaper, supported by the painted pink tones of '2411' by Flügger.

Above right. The entrance hall briefly pushes the apartment's palette to stronger extremes, with touches of red and turquoise on Jean Paul Gaultier's 'Hirondelles' wallpaper and coordinating tonal accents.

Opposite. The original white tiles from 1919 contrast with the delicate blue kitchen cabinetry creating a soft yet industrial look, while lighting and small accessories in blue create a playful game of hide-and-seek around the room.

Slashes of grey velvet curtains streaking
down the bedroom wall, the dark grey '5503'
paint by Flügger rising up the walls and the
'Mademoiselle' wallpaper artwork by Elitis are
all vivid points of difference to the bespoke
painted pink tones of Flügger's 'S0507R', a
gentle and welcoming take on monochrome.

Period tiles are paired with Sandberg's 'Chloé' wallpaper, forming a generation-jumping geometric effect in a mixed scale. The original terrazzo flooring was broken up, and replaced like-for-like by Copenhagen Terrazzo.

Do you have a favourite colour for the home?

The '4472' blue from Flügger – used in the living room here – has followed me for many years. I have painted cottages, former living rooms and also the hallway in that colour. I never get tired of it.

Are any hues banned from the house?

Colours that are completely saturated with pigment, and which are clear. I would never paint with primary colours, I just don't like them.

What's the easiest/cheapest/ quickest way to add colour to a home?

It has to be painting walls because it's such an easy thing to change, and it alters both the room's furniture and views.

Where do you visit for colour inspiration?

The Johannes Larsen Museum and Hay store in Copenhagen, and in Paris the Musée d'Orsay and Merci boutique.

Who are you following for interiors inspiration?

Artists Naja Tolsing (@najatolsing) and Signe Hom Berntsen (@signehomberntsen), designers Nynne Rosenvinge (@nynnerosenvinge) and Eline Engen (@elineengenhandmade), and stylist Sussie Frank (@sussiefrank).

Top tips for decorating with colour

1. Start by creating small islands of colour, painting just one wall or hanging a single piece of colourful art. You have to get used to it slowly.

2. It is important to repeat a colour several times in a room – bring in cushions, artwork …

3. Style colours with complementary tones, for example pink and green, or blue and yellow.

4. Think about letting a work of art define the colours in your rooms – start with the main colour in the work and repeat them in cushions, curtains or objects.

5. Get to know greyscale. Consider the degree of white and black in your chosen colour and how it affects the intensity of the colours.

CLAUDE

CARTIER

'Respect the history, but shake things up' were the instructions given to Claude Cartier, founder of French interior-design agency Claude Cartier Décoration, when she was handed the keys to an 18th-century mansion near Lyon in much need of a lick of paint and a heavy helping of modernity.

Claude's aesthetic is built around studying the architectural context of each project, unpicking the story of walls, tiles, ceilings and floors and weaving their history into a new aesthetic. 'I have a literary background and am instinctively attracted to designs rich in narrative,' she explains. 'We unfold stories within interiors.'

Reimagining such a magnificent home is no easy task, and honouring the past was high on Claude's must-do list. While rooms such as these are no stranger to colour, the modern makeover pushes the saturation level up a notch. 'Using colour in such a historic building is exciting, but a little daunting and dizzying,' says Claude. 'The tones must consider the history of the place while creating something fresh – it's like writing a new page of a book.'

Fashions were thrown out of the many windows – this is a property that will stand long after contemporary trends are gathering dust. The hues in the house invite exploration and pull you through each room, popping up in the most unexpected of spaces. The most adventurous use of paint is to be found lining the underside of the stairs, a life-like mural of blousy clouds quietly floating up to the next floor as if they've snuck in through the ceiling. 'The *trompe l'oeil* echoes the sky looming on the horizon,' says Claude. 'It's a modern take on classical painting.'

When you look at the borderline pastel palette of the house out of context, it may seem a little safe, but *au contraire* in situ. It's hard to find even one wall that takes its paint from a single can: 'I like to combine block colours so the wall interacts with itself,' explains Claude. 'It creates uniqueness as well as the illusion of volume.'

Almost every wall is striking and convention-breaking, many horizontally striped. The tricolour approach throughout incorporates period detailing and fresh plaster alike. In some rooms, the ceiling joins in the fun, its paint continuing down onto the walls making its opulent height seem a little less imposing. 'Nowhere was forbidden – we wanted to highlight the differences between the historic and the modern, real life and fantasy,' explains Claude.

While used in a daring way, the palette itself is gentle, chosen to accent and highlight the delicate period features and lightening the heaviness of the centuries-old space. Each wall has its own personality, but there are hues that pervade almost everywhere, tying the scheme together in a neat bow – bursts of sunny yellow, pinky-peach backdrops, pops of decadent Yves Klein blue and a whole bevy of paler sky shades. 'The tones are soft to underline

Previous page and left. Lined with the signature stripe-painted walls used throughout the house, the entrance makes a quiet, pastel-tinted statement drawing attention to the decorative panelling. The peach 'Blush RMDV41' by Ressource Paint paint tops the brand's blue 'Vent Ardoise I41' colour, drawing in the shades of a summer's sunset, which is echoed in the 'Slinkie Runner' by Patricia Urquiola at CC-Tapis.

the historic architecture, which always comes first,' says Claude. 'The colours – drunken pinks, milky blues – also correspond well to the soft lights and skies of the region.'

Claude's signature style wasn't always this way. For the first 20 years of her design career, her work was governed by beige, grey and white, before the risk-taker inside her broke free. 'I just felt a call to colour,' she says. 'I built a new design language for myself that was imbued with shades from around the globe.' Is there any turning back? 'I can't design a project without real colour,' she finishes. 'I want my spaces to feel bold, and colour creates an incredible energy as well as a joyful, creative audacity.'

Left. Climbing skywards, the painted cloudy mural on the stairs makes for a poetic ascent through the home. 'It's a nod to the historic *trompe l'oeil*,' says Claude. The original wooden panels were left unpainted as a reminder of the property's period origins.

Opposite. Playful flashes of modernity enter the home on the upper level, with a dazzling blue 'Bold' bench by Big-Game at Moustache and a pair of 'Palmette Lazer Cannon' rugs by CC-Tapis bringing in the big colour guns and contrasting with the original detailed woodwork. 'They create a new history for the house,' says Claude.

Saturated with sunny tones, the walls of the living room are painted in peach 'Blush RMDV41' and yellow 'Sienne RMDV30' by Ressource Paints, sandwiching a fresh slice of white between them. Curtains and rugs bring in additional shades that shift and dance, making them challenging to define.

Full of stormy shades, the snug is wrapped in a wave of deep blue velvet curtains, creating extravagance, texture and opulence. The 'Interior with Table' rug by Faye Toogood at CC-Tapis brings in other tones from around the house, while an intricate ceiling rose reminds us where we are.

'The painted horizontal bands compensate for the room's height, which could have felt too dizzying,' explains Claude of the dining room's rule-breaking walls. The eye is immediately drawn to the vivid yellow of the 'Malit' chairs by Gebrüder Thonet Vienna, which act as suns under the sky-blue ceiling of 'Enduit Romain Sans Nuage ER20' by Ressource Paints.

Pigment-rich bespoke blue
bedding by Claude Cartier
Décoration with Pierre Frey adds
punch to the surrounding softer
pastel tones in the bedroom, while
linear black details brings edge to
the gentle colour choices.

Do you have a favourite colour for the home?

'Green Cartier' a bespoke shade that I created for Ressource Paints.

Which colours do you like to combine?

Strong colours that could sometimes feel jarring – it's a modern, impactful way to approach colour.

Are any hues banned from the house?

I use very little red, as I find it one of the most difficult colours to work with. Maybe it will be an upcoming challenge!

Which space most benefits from colour?

The lobby. It's the first impression, the appetizer. And the first thing you see when you get home.

What's the easiest/cheapest/quickest way to add colour to a home?

Start with a work of art and build around it.

Have you had any decorating disasters?

Not yet ... fingers crossed!

Who are you following for interiors inspiration?

Colourist and designer Tekla Evelina Severin (@teklan), artist Justin Morin (@hellojustinmorin), rug brand CC-Tapis (@cc_tapis), architect and designer Dries Otten (@driesotten), designer India Mahdavi (@indiamahdavi), art director Giuliano Andrea dell'Uva (@giulianoandreadelluva).

Top tips for decorating with colour

1. Do not be afraid when working with colour – remember, it really is necessary.

2. Design colour along with the existing architecture of a building.

3. Remember the relationships between light and colour, and material and colour: matte and shiny materials express colours very differently, for example – they're interesting to play with.

4. Really design and plan your use of colour to fit with the type of building it's in.

5. Consider how colour affects atmosphere and how you want a space to feel.

FLEUR

DELESALLE

I nterior designer Fleur Delesalle aspires to one charming objective: 'to create harmony'. While as an aim this may seem simple, her work is anything but – a palette of colours, which range from the bright to the less-so, are deftly darned into delicate surrounds of pink-tinged white and neutral surfaces.

Her projects seek to create spaces that are on the same wavelength as each other yet with their own points of interest, while avoiding anything overly outlandish. Fleur compares her work to that of a make-up artist. 'Countless variations of white and beige are the "foundation" of all of my projects,' she explains. 'Then I add shadows, create breaks in the continuity of lines, and gradually add splashes of colour – a little green, a hint of pink ...'

If this 18th-century Parisian apartment is indeed now fully made-up, you can see how the balanced blend of the neutral and the bright is executed by a skilled, steady hand. Colour comes boldly but peacefully. Large vivid objects are deployed in simple, big spaces so their brightness is relaxed, while tones in smaller rooms are found in more delicate accent pieces, with both approaches surrounded by a sea of not-quite-whites, neutrals and more restful shades.

The palette depends on the location. 'My projects are inspired by their environment,' explains Fleur. 'This can be the colours in a garden or on Parisian roofs – nature and urban settings are equally important. In this home, the stone of the quays along the river gave me the shade for the walls, while the greens of nearby trees lead to a sofa, a tabletop and the bedroom and bathroom walls.'

The living areas are the main events, their creamy bases enlivened by rugs that knit abstract slices of pigment into their otherwise greyscale designs. Corresponding colours within the rooms bounce off these bases, a segment of rich peach carpet leading to a nearly-neon tangerine sofa as well as smaller, zesty orangey accents, while a mustard section of rug in the second living area paves the way for honey-hued chairs and gleaming gold details. Introducing similar tones on a mix of objects makes their entry into the space feel natural, pulling the look together easily and gracefully.

In the dining room the approach changes slightly. Underlined by neutrals – palest parquet and a barely-there paint – it's intricate and full of intrigue. Materials dance, forms repeat, textures play with light, and silhouettes undulate to build a colourless backdrop which insists that the eyes rove around it and ignore what really should be centre of attention: the hues built up in the middle. This island of colour mirrors the delicacy of what's around it but in an opposing way, vividity turned down a notch on what could be a bold, overbearing statement so the shades become soft, sugary and simple. The tabletop's oversized

Previous page. On first impression, this room is a free-for-all of unbounded brightness, but take a second look and its curated intent becomes apparent. A wall in a gentle white sets a soothing tone for a collection of mostly tonal shades, bolstered by the power of the orange 'Group Three Seat Sofa' by Philippe Malouin at SCP, which reverberate into the room through smaller pieces.

Opposite. A selection of large, statement slabs of colour has a transformative effect on the pale living room, the matching tones of the mustard vintage armchairs and fir-green 'Pumpkin' chair by Pierre Paulin creating a calm-yet-colourful feel.

slab of green is supported by ethereal glass lights draped with delicate *ombré* tones. The final effect? A sophisticated, creative take on colourful.

Upstairs the story evolves yet again — it's time for the walls to get involved. If downstairs is a newly primed, powdered and painted face, upstairs is a series of outfit changes, hinting at the palette used below but incorporating the tones with a more brazen style. 'They're different flavours,' explains Fleur. One bedroom and en-suite are dedicated to a sage-y mint, warmed with wood and freshened with white, another bedroom opts for apricot embellished with moments of monochrome, while a small mustard in-between space creates cosiness filled with a variety of natural browns and flashes of the bright.

Only the main bedroom strays away from all-over paint, opting only for a lipstick-like slash of red across its centre. 'As a primary colour, red wakes us up; it draws warmth to the space and it's provocative,' Fleur says. 'It also attracts light, which brings out all of its beauty, especially in the evening at sunset.'

For a home filled with such soul-enriching colour, it's strange to think that so much of it could be easily stripped back to neutral with just a bit of rearranging. The artistry with which it's all been brought together is the crux. Bold blocks of brightness can often seem as if they've landed in a space on a whim, often as single pieces chosen to be the star of the show, yet Fleur's colourful concoctions are complex room recipes — everything there for a reason and working hard for its spot. 'Colour is expression,' Fleur states. 'It is an ode to the joy of life, an invitation to feel cheerful.' But there's a caveat: 'Beware: colour can kill colour, so less is more!'

Left. While the materiality of the timber and terrazzo dominate the kitchen, the simple green table — a bespoke design by Fleur — has a metamorphic effect on the room, adding vitality and life as well as pointing to the subtle shades in Max Lamb's 'Marmoreal' engineered marble surface on the island.

Opposite. Fleur's bespoke lacquered marble-topped table creates a bang in the dining room. The 'Phenomena' pendant lights by Studio Dechem at Bomma echo and exaggerate the tones that surround them.

Above. A dusty peach hue wraps around one of the bedrooms, celebrated by soft-toned wood and contrasted with moments of monochrome.

Opposite. The dual-purpose headboard both envelops the sleeper and creates an office space, a bespoke design by Fleur. Patchwork cushions by India Mahdavi chime with the rich shade, while Kartell's 'Componibili' tables by Anna Castelli Ferrieri add a grungy green contrast.

Opposite. An ode to nature, the bathroom fuses tangy mint walls and matching bespoke marble with timber surfaces, with slashes of white making it feel clean and contemporary.

Above. With a rich green drawing the eye up the high walls of the guest bedroom, a pale waterfall of white curtains simultaneously brings the ceiling down into the room. Natural accents create an indoor–outdoor feel.

minik
ans, Before Robots: Top 10
n Stories

Wystawa potrwa do 17 listopada 2016 roku | www.kasiamichalski.com

Do you have a favourite colour for the home?

Sweet-related shades such as marzipan, powdery Turkish Delight pink and salted-butter caramel are the perfect allies for my projects. The Calisson d'Aix candy from Aix-en-Provence is a decorating delight – matte ivory icing sugar with faded yellow.

What's the best way to bring colour inside?

Fabrics are very important for introducing colour into a project – the sofa, the upholstery of a chair seat, etc, as well as rugs and carpets.

What are your key materials to decorate with?

I am drawn to all natural materials, from wood to stone. It's really exciting to work in a way that matches what those materials can offer.

Are any hues banned from the house?

I'm afraid of grey and I don't like black except when it emphasises a shape or outlines a perspective. I was afraid of blue too, then I 'faced' it and I'm very, very happy with the result, so never say never.

Where do you visit for colour inspiration?

Villa Necchi Campiglio in Milan, Villa Majorelle in Marrakech, Luis Barragán's projects in Mexico and Ricardo Bofill's Walden 7 in Barcelona.

Top tips for decorating with colour

1. Never have pure white walls – yes to colours or off-white!

2. Get colours to interact with each other, for example replicate a shade in a rug elsewhere in the room.

3. Woods are beautiful when they tend towards warm golden hues, but not when they go grey or greenish.

4. Energise nuanced and subtle colours like khaki, rust and off-white with a splash of strong and saturated colour.

5. Banish grey!

'This teaspoon of mustard acts as an "airlock" between two rooms,' explains Fleur. 'It plays its role as a hyphen between the two – an off-white would have been too banal.'

GCG

ARCHITECTES

When you think of a home decorated with nature-inspired hues, the varied scheme of this house isn't what would typically spring to mind. A chorus of colours conducted by French architecture and interior-design practice GCG Architectes, the wide-ranging shades in this classical Parisian apartment are pulled directly from the outdoors with a bold, playful, experimental approach.

'We are super colourful and we love all colours from pastels to brights – we use an original mix-and-match of materials and shades drawn from nature,' explains GCG Architectes' founder Olivia Charpentier. 'If something works outside, it will work inside. We look to landscapes, plants or animals – the palette always fits.' If you're still unsure about what to add to your blank slate first, Olivia advises you consider what mood you want to capture, or activities that make you happy. 'Think about what you are looking for in your life. Joy? Calm? Travel? Comfort? Let that direct your choice of colours.'

The starting point for the firm was a sea of Parisian parquet and the desire to form a retreat from the hectic city outside. Then came the green-ness that flourishes throughout the space, supported by understated pale walls, speaking of soothing forests and flowers as well as acting as an *au naturel* base for the other more intrepid shades that followed. 'Yves Saint Laurent said that all greens work together, and it's quite true,' says Olivia. 'Green is often a colour you don't think about – it's more of an emotion or feeling you have that reminds you of nature.'

The expedition begins in the hallway, where an overhead canopy of trees and leaves wallpapered onto the ceiling narrates the departure from urban jungle into something with more of a holiday feel, setting the tone for a home that celebrates Earth's bounty in an unexpected, unconventional way 'Paris is a stressful environment,' explains Olivia. 'We seek to create a different universe – somewhere to escape to.'

If there's one word that sums up this property, it's *contrast*: historic meets contemporary, rich pigments sit alongside the subtle, gloss shares a roller with emulsion, black accents oppose white as urban melts into rural. 'We love to play and challenge the story of a place,' says Olivia. 'We wanted a space that was dynamic and fun as well as embracing the outdoors in a delicate, poetic way.'

What distinguishes the palette of the home is its eyebrow-raising colour combinations, which are at once dominating and cleverly understated. Thus, towering over the living room is a bookshelf painted in a dazzling high-gloss orange to draw in and reflect the light of the sun, while the shelves within are coated in a faintest of the faint matte pink which offers a tactile point of difference and a sense of warm stillness. 'The orange is a joyful visual

Previous page. A sweeping arc upholstered in Manuel Canovas' 'Bellevue' fabric mirrored by a matching carpet plays with tactility, and the tone coordinates with sections of the 'Upanayana WP' wallpaper by James Malone Fabrics.

Opposite. While an orange full-height, built-in shelf may sound scary on paper, GCG Architectes have executed it with a delicate, considered touch, choosing a shade straight from a summer evening sky. The juicy paint colour, 'Venezia' by Clay, has a high gloss finish which is juxtaposed with matte shelves painted in the warm pale pink of Little Greene's 'Julie's Dream'.

tonic that brings you closer to the sun and to the light, whereas the soft pink adds sweetness and a romantic pop,' smiles Olivia. 'Texture and colour contrasts bring so much personality to a home.' The pale pinkness spread from the shelves onto the main walls, its blink-and-you'll-miss-it tone bringing a quiet cosiness to the space. 'I couldn't help but put it everywhere!' Olivia says.

The kitchen plays the game of contrasts too, the cabinets an outspoken shade of fresh green evoking herbs and meadows, the room finished with with raspberry-tinted floral upholstery, for a strolling through a field feel..

Perhaps the boldest colour duo can be found in the bedrooms, which work with pastel aqua and flamingo hues at varying levels of bravery. The shelves see a slick of not-quite-red pink shimmying along their inner edge, and on the outer edge a high-gloss channel houses an electric filament that audaciously contradicts the pale calmness of the room's main tone. 'The green-blue brings a uniformity, a continuity to the house, while the pink adds rock'n'roll!' says Olivia. Bedroom number two takes a different approach, demonstrating the power of textured colour with a reddish velvet carpet, as well as flirting with snippets of the same tone within its blue-backed wallpaper. 'The soft headboard and carpet capture light and soothe the pinky pigment,' explains Olivia. 'This bedroom feels sweet and comfortable.'

'Colour is life,' asserts Olivia. 'It brings joy and light and rhythm, allowing you to take ownership of your home so it can tell the story of your personality, like a portrait. Every tone you choose affects your emotions – brights will create dynamism, while softer shades are calmer and more contemplative.' It seems the trick, cheerfully achieved here, is mastering how to balance both at once.

Left. The overall colourlessness of the living room offers visual respite in the home, the tiled floor by the window designed to support real-life potted greenery. Rattan birds take flight on bespoke screens designed by GCG Architectes and made by the French artist François Passolunghi. 'We love contrasting materials as well as colours,' says Olivia. 'Here the walls are matte and the ceiling is shiny.'

Opposite. Upon entering the apartment, you are greeted by the open sky of Ananbô's 'Udaipur' wallpaper, and the landscape feel is supported by the verdant shade of Farrow & Ball's 'Calke Green', which is painted onto the surrounding cupboards. 'Walking into the hallway is like looking up in a jungle – it's a serene natural roof,' says Olivia. 'You leave the urban life behind as soon as you open the door, entering into a quiet place within the forest.'

The kitchen's take on green is refreshing and light. Farrow & Ball's 'Calke Green' paint works with the glass and mirrors on the cabinets, with the fanciful florals of the 'Mademoiselle Jouanon' pattern by Pierre Frey layering in detail and interest. 'My advice for choosing a kitchen colour? You can't go wrong if you pick a very fresh shade from nature,' advises Olivia.

Little Greene's 'Cape Red' paint links this bathroom to its adjoining bedroom, with green-tinted waxed concrete walls hinting at the apartment's key colour. Monochrome details link back to the rest of the house and are crowned with a black ceiling designed to evoke the feeling of night.

Do you have a favourite colour for the home?

'Orange Aurora' by Little Greene – it's a coral orange which is very cheerful and warm. I really love it.

Which colours do you like to combine?

Green and pink! They're found so often in nature, you can't go wrong pairing these two in any shades.

Are any hues banned from the house?

No. All colours are beautiful, it just depends on what they are mixed with.

Which space most benefits from colour?

I like colour in small spaces where it is enveloping and creates a total change of scenery.

Do you have a colour motto?

Look at what you like to wear and put it on the wall!

Where do you visit for colour inspiration?

The Centre Pompidou to look at the paintings.

Who are you following for interiors inspiration?

Artist João Incerti (@o_incerti), rug designer Marguerite Le Maire (@marguerite_le_maire), mosaic artist Sika Viagbo (@atelier_lilikpo), eco paint brand Argile (@argilepeinture), interior designer Kelly Wearstler (@kellywearstler) and creatives Marie Kalt (@marie_kalt), Cristina Celestino (@cristinacelestino) and India Mahdavi (@indiamahdavi).

What are your colour goals for future projects?

I want to create a pink façade for a building – light bubblegum pink full of enthusiasm and joy.

Top tips for decorating with colour

1. Just go for it – be daring! You can always change something.
2. Base the palette of your home around an artwork you love, or your fashion sense.
3. Pair matte and high-shine finishes for contrast.
4. Add in small touches of darkness to make colour pop.
5. Paint or decorate your ceiling – it elevates a space fantastically.

'In this space we needed some excitement and dynamism,' explains Olivia. Little Greene's 'Cape Red' competes for attention with the cooler 'Bleu Persan' by Argile, both paints harmonising with the graphic 'Promenade au Faubourg' wallpaper by Hermès that draws the focal point together.

GUNTER

& CO

If there's one tone that Irene Gunter, creative director and founder of London-based interior-design and architecture firm Gunter & Co, relies on, it's black. The studio's entire palette is based around it. In the majority of her projects it features in every room, present on every wall – albeit just small a dash of it mixed into all of her key colour choices.

These shadowy, black-tinged shades are partly an antidote to the moody British weather – so often cloudy and overcast – which Irene combats by creating warm, cosy, spaces draped in colour that slowly seeps both into the room and its occupants, and partly it's down to the surprising mood these slightly sullied tones prompt. 'My palette is a little bit dirty, a little bit muddied,' she describes. 'So even if the colours are quite strong, deep or vibrant, the black tint makes the home feel very soft and approachable.' A bold tone plus blackness may seem like the recipe for a somewhat scary space, but this is very much not the case with these enveloping, dark-edged hues, which feel more akin to wrapping yourself in a thick blanket.

While Gunter & Co's brief in this central London maisonette was to do what they thought best, the scheme was really dictated by the levels of light, which is very low in most rooms. While instinct may insist that the darker the area, the paler it should be, Irene says otherwise (she says it frequently, to a lot of disbelieving people). 'It's a common mistake – if there's not a great deal of light in a space, there's not much point trying to go bright and white because it will still feel dark and dingy,' she explains 'Go strong with the colour choices – even a medium saturation level will make everything feel much more comfortable because the light gets absorbed and the room will give you back a much softer atmosphere which is a nicer environment to be in. Work with the light levels rather than against them!'

And so, the home's colour palette was decided upon by the movement of the London sun. 'A lot of the rooms don't get a great deal of daylight, so we needed to play quite heavily with colour to make them feel vibrant and interesting,' Irene says. Thus, downstairs, the dim living room was doused in a deep green and brightened with coordinating paler tones with the meeting point between the living room and kitchen supervised by a fireplace that transitions the walls from dark to light. Upstairs, the shady, completely enclosed bathroom was metamorphosed by a cheerful, enlivening mustard, while the sunlit main bedroom was given the least amount of richness.

Irene's approach is about colour exploration in a thoughtful, methodical way, combining hues with light to create spaces you want to nestle into yourself. 'In the place where you live, colour needs to have some restorative qualities where it makes you feel calm and at ease in your surroundings,' she explains. 'We always opt

A bespoke Gunter & Co-designed fireplace marks the transition from living room to kitchen, from dark to light, turning the living room's green wall into a statement art piece.

for colour and contrast where we can, but it's in moderation, not on every surface, and never "more is more".' These considered, tonal shades go hand in hand with elegant materials – herringbone floors, panelled walls – and tactile finishes – stone, velvet, glass, leather – that provide moments of respite from what could be all-consuming pigment.

White is also omnipresent – never a focus but always hovering nearby waiting to form a pause in the palette, or guide the gaze from space to space. 'Dipping a whole room in a colour can feel very intense and overpowering, which can really work in some properties but, in general, if you just pile colour onto colour it doesn't have a chance to breathe,' Irene says. 'It's nice for the eye to have some restful points to land on, and whiteness also boosts the vibrancy of the tones around it.'

For Irene, decorating with colour is inextricably linked with wellbeing, and her homes feel like entering a world where all there is to do is sink into the soothing shades. 'The more comfortable and confident you can be with colour, the more your home will reward you for it,' she says. 'Colour can make a house feel softer and more welcoming, a space that you genuinely want to spend time in and that elevates you rather than draining energy – you want your home to feel like a nice big hug when you come home.'

'Green calms you down and puts you at ease; it's friendly, which is obviously something that you'd want to encourage in a living room,' says Irene of the walls painted in Farrow & Ball's 'Green Smoke'. The one-colour palette is used in a relatively small space so it doesn't overwhelm, with metallic brass accents adding richness and warmth.

As the ceiling was fairly low in the spare bedroom, it was painted the same shade of 'Setting Plaster' by Farrow & Ball as the walls, 'otherwise you'd have this stubby, short little wall, which would then be clearly delineated from a white ceiling', explains Irene. 'Painting it all the same made the room seem taller.' Greens and pinks were mixed to create a relaxed informality.

'I wanted the red spare bedroom to have its own story to tell rather than just being a version of another room,' Irene says of the space fully drenched in '1-024' by Papers and Paints. 'As it is a guest bedroom, so not for the owners to be spending lots of time in, we could have a little bit of fun and use a more stimulating colour.'

Opposite. The light-filled main bedroom can carry paler tones than the rest of the house, the sun accentuating subtle textures. 'I wanted to use a brighter colour palette to make the most of the light,' Irene explains. 'The room has a different feel, perhaps a little bit more grown up.'

Above. Irene pulled out tones from the bath, wrapped in '003 Ottanio' fabric by Brochier, to colour the rest of the space. 'The textile combined colours that I wouldn't normally put together, but it worked in the bigger space surrounding it,' she says. 'The colours loosen up the traditional fittings and make them less serious.'

What's the best way to bring colour inside?

I'd rather have the background be colourful than the added details, which is probably the exact opposite of how most people would do it, so colourful walls and architectural woodwork, more neutral upholstered items.

How do you approach accessorising colourfully?

With artwork. Take a really colourful print – it doesn't have to be expensive – then work onwards from that, pulling out colours from it for throws, cushions, vases, ceramics to add personality.

How would you name your own paint range?

I'd go fun and have a paint colour called 'Yesterday's Hangover', or another one called 'My Mother-in-law'.

Where do you visit for colour inspiration?

The Lime Wood Hotel in the New Forest, UK, designed by Susie Atkinson. I love going there and just looking at the colours and just thinking 'How did she put all of this together?'

Who are you following for interiors inspiration?

I follow quite a few American interior designers because they're bold with their use of colour, including Stephen Gambrel (@stevengambrel), Stephanie Sabbe (@sabbeinteriordesign), Kelly Wearstler (@kellywearstler) and Sheila Bridges (@harlemtoilegirl).

Top tips for decorating with colour

1. Always look at which way the room faces first to assess the light.

2. Judge your ceiling heights. If you're trying to make the room feel less imposing, maybe bring the ceiling down or if it's a really cosy space decide on how to tie in the woodwork.

3. Think about bringing period mouldings out in a different colour, whether it's a subtle difference or a bigger contrast, as this can really add to the architectural detailing of a room.

4. Be brave with your window colour. Darker window frames draw the eye out whereas white frame make you visually stop so you don't take in the exterior as much. It's nice to add colour – we've got navy frames, dark green frames …

5. Play with realistically sized samples – a tiny paint swatch is not helpful. We paint them onto a big piece of board and carry it into different areas and lights.

ATELIER

ND INTERIOR

When endless expanses of lilac walls are the last thing you notice in a room – if you register them at all – you know you're in a home that means business with colour. Designed by Nicole Dohmen, founder of Dutch design practice Atelier ND Interior, there is not a jot of white paint to be seen in this 1918 brownstone, set in the countryside near Amsterdam.

'We all get really serious when it comes to decorating – we are much too safe,' says Nicole. 'I think many people style their homes for other people, and you have to have a lot of nerve to choose bold colours.' Hurling caution and solemnity into the wind, Nicole fashions spaces that fall spectacularly on the stylish side of psychedelic, where there's no such thing as greyscale and pastel palettes are *passé*. 'I find boldness with soft combinations incredibly beautiful' she says. 'Bold colours in the same shade, or with the same heaviness, become too overpowering and loud – it's a bit screamy.' Instead, the paint chart is reimagined – pale pigments become neutrals, soft tones that would be a feature for most are a comforting middle ground, and vivid hues are well-timed punchlines finishing each scheme with flamboyance. 'It's like a puzzle,' explains Nicole. 'I get into the zone and it all comes together.'

The house is a lesson on how to bring the rainbow indoors in a sophisticated, non-children's-colouring-book way – a careful balancing act struck by a measured combination of the bright and the not-so: red comes as an accent and in a variety of textures, a crimson lamp base here, a candy stripe there; a yellow handrail bounces off warm timber stairs; pink is sprinkled throughout, at once a background colour and the main event; green is used sparingly in all guises, from sharp kiwi to mossy grass shades; orange is embraced as a natural tone, mimicking sunlight or as flowers or fruit; purple drifts in a haze, pastel walls supporting richer shades of plum; and tiny flashes of blue at the corner of your vision complete the spectrum.

Nicole worked closely with the owner, actor Carice van Houten, whose eclectic and unrestrained style pushed colour boundaries to the extreme and laughed in the face of the rule book. 'Carice wanted a lot of colour, but with an edge so it didn't all fit together,' explains the designer. 'She didn't want it too neat or perfect.' So, when a scheme seemed finished, Carice would mix in a clashing or unexpected hue via vintage 1960s furniture, a piece by a contemporary Dutch designer or a fabric that had caught her eye. 'We had a lot of things to combine – the trick was getting the home to flow with all the different colours and blend the styles without making it look totally crazy,' recounts Nicole. The result combines a trip to the circus with an afternoon at an art gallery, a controlled explosion of 'ooh' and 'aah'-worthy tones.

Previous page. Lined with deep plum custom Tadelakt plaster, Kelly Wearstler's 'Hex' wallpaper, a vivid yellow bannister painted in RAL '1027 Curry' and clashing purple door metalwork in '4004 Claret Violet', the entrance hall introduces the home with a bang. 'When you walk into the house you're instantly amazed,' smiles Nicole. 'It's a wow moment.'

To fit it all in, rooms developed their own aesthetic, with paint and wallpaper envoking a different atmosphere behind each door. 'Every room has an individual personality,' explains Nicole. 'Sometimes you need quieter spaces in your life as well as the more lively.' While areas traditionally devoted to relaxation would echo their function in their palette, and those designated for daytime activities and social events would be brighter and more vibrant, not so chez Carice. The standout non-conformist in the house has to be the spare bedroom, bedecked head-to-toe in a mind-bending multicoloured meadow which is playfully reinforced by grassy green carpet. Accessorised with shots of primary shades, you're guaranteed a night of vivid dreams.

The key to resplendent colour indoors, it seems, is a potent potion of planning and spontaneity. While Nicole and Carice depended on thoroughly prepared mood boards and samples to guide their way, they also allowed themselves to instinctually fall in love with swatches and design objects, and to absorb new finds into their plan. 'Houses that are colourful in such a personal way are so alive,' says Nicole. 'They really lift you up.'

Bespoke blush-pink paint by LJM Studio creates a neutral backdrop to the living room's theatrical palette. The space's lead colours come from stars of the show: a kiwi-toned 'Milano' sofa by Paola Navone for Baxter, a red-tinged vintage 'Soriana' sofa by Afra and Tobia Scarpa for Cassina and a tan armchair from Siton Vintage, the rich plum rug by Kvadrat bonding all four tones while smaller pieces add shots of brightness and pattern. Carice captured the room's eclectic colours and added more with a figurative artwork by Peggy Kuiper.

Opposite. Nicole's mantra of 'lilac is the new white' is nowhere more apparent than in the dining room, the pretty purple hue tinting almost every surface. Pale in comparison to the rest of the space, the sculptural pink table by Sabine Marcelis and vanilla-toned 'Pigreco' chairs by Tobia Scarpa at Gavina stand out, illuminated by incoming shafts of daylight.

Above. In the planning stages, the kitchen went through many colour iterations until brown tiles by Intercodam and cabinets painted in 'Invisible Green' by Little Greene and 'Mouse's Back' by Farrow & Ball were settled on. 'We needed a more natural colour so the space wasn't too poppy,' explains Nicole. 'This space is the neutral area of the house.' Never fear though, there's brightness if you know where to look for it – the drawers and cupboards are lined with bright yellow.

Opposite. The walls painted in moody 'Pontefract' by Paint & Paper Library plunge you into darkness as you enter the main bedroom, pulling the spacious room inwards and creating cosiness. The kiwi carpet by M.I.D. Carpets adds to the 1970s vibe of the house and nods to the coordinating sofa downstairs, while the curtains in Zoffany's 'Abstract 1928' fabric are a geometric summary of the space's scheme.

Favourite colour for the home?

'Setting Plaster' and 'Mizzle' from Farrow & Ball, and 'Pink Soon' and 'Sahara Sand' by File Under Pop. I love light airy colours that are not too serious.

Which space most benefits from colour?

The living room and the library – I love it when these rooms have an outspoken or rich colour.

What's the easiest/cheapest/ quickest way to add colour to a home?

Colourful tablecloths, cushions and throws. I also like to frame fabric.

How do you approach accessorising colourfully?

When the base colours in the room are quiet, pump up the volume with some crazy objects in different sizes and some wild colours.

Do you have a colour motto?

Don't add too many bold colours together. Try to start with a base colour like a soft blush, soft yellows, soft greens and add extra colours.

Where do you visit for colour inspiration?

My most recent inspiration trip was to the beautiful Yves Saint Laurent exhibition at the Centre Pompidou in Paris. I am always inspired by art.

Who are you following for interiors inspiration?

Creative Jenna Lyons (@jennalyonsnyc), art space Dimore Gallery (@dimoregallery), design magazine Architectural Digest (@archdigest), interior designer Kelly Wearstler (@kellywearstler) and design and interiors-led Instagrammer Marc Costa (@m.a.r.c.c.o.s.t.a)

Top tips for decorating with colour

1. Don't be afraid. Please just do. Life is too short.

2. Let's have fun and start with the first colour that makes your heart tick. Don't take it all so seriously!

3. Make it personal. It is your home and if yellow is your favourite colour, search for your perfect yellow.

4. At first the paint can look 'wow' and be in your face too much – give it time and always have the end result in mind.

5. When you are coming out of the construction phase and everything is white, pink might seem a bit too much, especially with all the builders walking around. Stick to your plan and be secure about your choices!

'When we saw the "Hollyhocks" wallpaper by House of Hackney, we said "Let's go crazy!"', explains Nicole. 'We chose the grassy green carpet because we thought it was amusing with the florals. It may seem wild, but when you're in the room it's just so much fun.'

NANNA CECILIA

REICHSTEIN-HENRIKSEN

Folded into the forest of coastal town Gilleleje in Denmark, is the effervescent summerhouse of Nanna Cecilia Reichstein-Henriksen, founder of digital vintage shop Sentaku, which acts as a store for the plethora of old-school interiors goodies she can't help but pick up in Scandinavia's flea markets, fairs and auction houses. 'It's somewhere between a disease and an interest,' she smiles. 'I just can't keep all of the things I find.'

The home is a glorious mish-mash of colour and pattern, the contrast and variety at once an outburst of energy while also maintaining a balanced, calming museum-like feel thanks to the house's crisp grey backdrop. 'I would recommend anyone who wants to live with colour, to start with a soft grey on the walls, because it looks really beautiful with other shades,' says Nanna. 'It's a calm base which feels homely, and creates more interest than boring white.'

Once the timber walls, floor and ceiling were painted in Farrow & Ball's 'Elephant's Breath', then came the excitement. Every colour of the rainbow intersects in clashing patterns, with vivid artworks, expressive textiles and unique vintage finds at every turn. Neon blazes, florals befriend stripes and checks, and an army of accessories battle for attention. At Nanna's, there are no rules. 'I don't have any boundaries and I hate matching,' she says. 'The more something doesn't go together, the more I like it – it's fun, it's wild and it creates an atmosphere of rule breaking and partying, a vibrant feeling like you're doing something wrong and you almost think "Is that legal?"!'

You are welcomed into the chromatic getaway via a nondescript entrance-slash-boot room, the demure pink-tinted chandelier a small hint at the minor mayhem that is to ensue. Progress into the next chamber – the open-plan living/dining/kitchen space – and any colourless expectations are quickly forgotten. There's no intense main event that draws the eye; instead, the space is dappled with brightness at every turn, inviting exploration and discovery. What is that vivacious set of artworks surrounding the bedroom door? Let's go and see. Is that green silk pendant a light or a decoration? Not sure. That looks like a fluorescent Tom Dixon 'Offcut' stool peeking from behind the grey sofa ... It is.

If there's one element that defines the home, it's the multicoloured textiles. Cushions have quietly taken over – two, three, four, five of which are piled every which way you look, creating plush pockets of playfulness. 'I have a thing for cushions,' Nanna admits. 'I think we have 30 in a range of old and modern textiles.' They come in squared and elongated forms, in illustrative and geometric prints and in rich and faded hues. Each design has its own personality – of course, absolutely no two are the same. Along with the carefree feel these non-coordinated tones bring to the house, they also say 'Come, sit with me,' 'Go on, put your feet up,' and 'Did you just spill something? That's ok.'

While small objects – art, fabrics, lighting, rugs and second-hand finds – are psychedelic, dramatic and cheerful, the larger pieces of furniture err towards the conventional including Scandinavian design old and new in natural timbers, leathers and weaves. 'I want quality furniture that lasts a long time,' Nanna explains. 'The things that I'm going to keep for many years I try to make calmer and classic – they can always be decorated and updated with a colourful new cushion or a fun candlestick.' The kitchen is a pigmented point of difference, painted in a warm brick-red tone. 'It's both crazy and calm at the same time,' she says. 'The paint has a lot of black in it, so the redness pops, as well as being relaxing to look at and feeling traditional – it's about using bright colours in a soft way.'

This is a happy-go-lucky, free-spirited house. Who cares if others don't understand it? Nanna uses the colours she is instinctually drawn to – powerful pinks, blues, greens, yellows and oranges that would usually compete for dominance. But somehow here they click – apparently, if you get enough bold shades together, they'll eventually form a team, the brighter tones melding into one sweeping layer of playful vividness. 'I don't take myself that seriously and I don't think my home should either,' Nanna says. 'I think for other people it's like going into something wild, but these colours are my mental treat – they make me feel calm and safe, and reflect who I am, and my family. When I walk in, they put a smile on my face.'

A pair of colour-contrasting Danish fold-out beds from the 1970s fill the children's room. 'I was searching online for something a bit playful and different,' says Nanna. 'They didn't match – which is very uncommon – so I was happy!

132

The open-plan main space takes in the dining alcove, living area and kitchen. The decoration is the same jumble of vivid shades and dulled vintage colours on a grey backing, throughout. 'I didn't have a big plan for the décor, it was more intuitive – it just came to me,' says Nanna.

Mixing clashing fabrics is something of a speciality of Nanna's; 'I love it, it's challenging and feels almost like it's unacceptable and not very responsible,' she says. 'It makes me happy not to be very grown up.' The cushions are a mix from Svenkst Tenn, Maria La Rosa and Aiayu.

The calm entrance is coated in grey
'Elephant's Breath' paint by Farrow & Ball.
'We knew that we were going to add a lot of
splashy colour, so we painted the house all
one tone to tie it together,' explains Nanna.

The existing Ikea kitchen was enlivened with a rusty red coat of Farrow & Ball's 'Picture Gallery' paint. 'We wanted to make it a little more modern and more "us",' explains Nanna. The 1970s bamboo serving trolley is another Danish flea-market find.

Do you have a favourite colour for the home?

I cannot have a home without something – big or small – in bright, postbox red. It's a positive colour, a little over the top and a little too much – it reflects how I am.

What's the easiest/cheapest/quickest way to add colour to a home?

The first thing I would recommend would be to go out and find a nice old quilt and cushions to get some colours in – it's cheaper than buying art, a really easy way to add colour.

Do you have a colour motto?

Don't be too 'correct' in how you approach your home.

How do you approach accessorising colourfully?

Cushions and textiles – they are a nice, cheap way to upgrade your home with colours. And don't be afraid to buy a lampshade that doesn't match the foot of the lamp, it's less boring when they don't go together.

Where do you visit for colour inspiration?

I love the La Colombe d'Or hotel in the South of France, it's very old school, but the way it uses colour is amazing.

Who are you following for interiors inspiration?

Creative Nadia Olive Schnack (@nadiaoliveschnack), interior designers Joanna Plant (@joannaplantinteriors), Rosanna Bossom (@rosannabossomltd) and Alice Keswick (@alicekeswickinteriors) and art space Dimore Gallery (@dimoregallery).

Top tips for decorating with colour

1. Buy colours that make you happy and feel good.
2. Start with colourful accessories.
3. Make small galleries of different types of art hanging together.
4. Don't be afraid of doing something out of your comfort zone.
5. If you like it, then you can do it.

The bedroom's main attraction is a vintage patchwork quilt, full of history and portions of brightness – yet another flea-market bargain. The tightly striped blue-and-red wallpaper above the bed clashes with the yellow design to the left (both are from Tapet-Café) – 'that clash feels so politically incorrect, we had to do it,' says Nanna.

KINGSTON LAFFERTY

DESIGN

The universe of Róisín Lafferty, founder and creative director of Irish interior-design house Kingston Lafferty Design, is quite literally rose tinted. Known for dousing rooms in colour — walls, floors, doors, ceilings and decorative detailing — Róisín's palette is one of free-spirited whimsy, with smoky pink-tinged tones that invoke an air of the dreamlike. 'We use paint to create an all-encompassing cloud of romanticism,' she explains. 'It takes you to another world.'

Step into this dusky palette and you'll come across colour combinations that in any other tonal approach might be overwhelming, yet, with a layer of foggy mist over them, they turn into a sea of calmness. 'We are unafraid of colour,' Róisín explains. 'We play with contrasts, merging different tones that don't naturally go together — there's a fine line where it almost clashes. Sometimes, that's where the beauty can be found.' Elements of the unexpected are at the core of the studio's approach, and while their interiors include a wide spectrum of hues, they are ushered in with whispers, considerately and calmly. 'We aim to surprise, but it's subtle,' she continues. 'We don't want someone to walk in and for their senses to be assaulted; it should be gradual, a haze they're drawn into that balances boldness and detail with serenity and atmosphere.'

For Kingston Lafferty Design, colouring a home is an all-or-nothing affair, and areas that are habitually left white or overlooked are welcomed into its paint-covered realm. 'I hate when you walk into a room which has powerful painted walls, but then the ceiling and the skirting are white — the contrast practically shouts,' says Róisín. 'It's the same with doors. People will say "Oh, I couldn't possibly paint the doors," but what they don't often look at is the tone of the wood — sometimes, when you step back, doors have an orange tint which, once you've noticed, you can't unsee. Unpainted areas like these form blocks in the room and the eye is distracted and doesn't know what to focus on. Do you want the room's feature to be the woodwork and ceiling? Probably not. Painting them, even in a neutral shade, stops them being highlighted as different — it will instantly change how you think about colour.'

Creating interiors that evoke curiosity and a sense of the child-like, Róisín's work is suffused with nostalgia, transporting you to a place with a vague sense of familiarity, filled with candy floss, languorous summer days and laughter floating on the breeze. 'It's about walking in and being completely enveloped in warmth and softness, like the colours are caressing you,' she says.

A sense of playfulness is immediately apparent in this Victorian home, tucked unassumingly in the Dublin suburbs. Upon entry, it's obvious that things are not as conventional as the traditional architecture may have had you believe. Grey-tinged pinks immediately surround you,

Simple geometric pieces in solid block colours establish a child-like theme, with richly pigmented colours adding an all-grown-up twist. 'We wanted it to be sophisticated — there's a lot of different colours but they all have a muddiness to them,' explains Róisín. 'It's a humorous take on a formal Victorian room.' The house's two fireplaces provide light relief in cheeky, non-19th century shades.

The ceiling was — surprisingly — left in a pale tone to accentuate the painted cornicing and ceiling rose. 'Normally we would blend it all in, but we wanted to create something more graphic and strong with the architectural feature,' explains Róisín.

ushering you into the house as if letting you into a secret. Meandering from room to room feels like an adventure, and there's a lot to discover. The living room is like a toybox, filled with a sculptural pick-and-mix of almost-bright blocky furniture that you want to take hold of and show your friends. Fireplaces are resplendent in blush, lemon and green, a neon yellow line pulls you around the kitchen, a golden archway becomes a portal to the bedroom and ornate original features come in a muted rainbow of shades. 'I saw the architecture as a canvas,' affirms Róisín. 'Painting in the coving, ceiling roses and the period detailing made it look like icing on a cake.' Did we slip through that peach-tinted looking-glass in the entrance?

Róisín's soft palette permeates not only the walls (and ceilings), but the very essence of the home, as if each surface was painted with an emotion. 'Our tones are playful and whimsical, not at all serious, formal or stuffy – we have fun and experiment with our homes, filling them with the unexpected,' says Róisín. 'Colour has such an important role in how people feel – our palette is based on mood, dulled down to create a low-key, social atmosphere suitable for interiors. You can see people's body language actually change as they walk in and are enveloped by it.'

Left. The hallway was designed to evoke the feel of putting on rose-tinted glasses: Pantone's smoky pink 'Mahogany Rose' paint creates a soothing and light-hearted atmosphere, and a peach-tinted mirror adds to the warming effect. 'It's romantic and inviting,' says Róisín. 'It's playful and childlike, without being sickly, sweet or sugary.'

Opposite. Diamond-patterned storage painted in Farrow & Ball's green-tinged 'Castle Gray' run through the living rooms, simple childish shapes that are mirrored in the fireplaces and emphasise the pattern of the parquet. The room is almost dedicated to one colour, as Róisín chose to limit its tones to highlight the natural light that pours in.

Above. Three-dimensional 'Rombini' tiles by Ronan & Erwan Bouroullec for Mutina add a slice of brightness to the recent kitchen extension by NOJI Architects, the pale blueness dancing with the built-in yellow cabinet detail.

Entered via a stately gold-lined archway, the bedroom is a world unto itself, filled with more soothing tones and textures than downstairs. 'I love the idea of actually stepping through into another dimension. We wanted this space to be absolutely tranquil,' says Róisín. 'Subconsciously stepping through a portal into a different zone creates distance from the rest of the house'.

Do you have a favourite colour for the home?

'Green Smoke' by Farrow & Ball. It just works with every type of architecture and always has a sophisticated serenity.

What's the best way to bring colour inside?

With marble, which I'm obsessed with. With natural materials you can bring in colour as much as you like – it doesn't date.

Which space most benefits from colour?

The entrance hallways – they create the first impression of any home and are a great way of introducing people to the overall feel of the house.

Have you had any decorating disasters?

Many! If I didn't, I wouldn't be taking any risks. Just recently we had to repaint a huge section of a house because the colour looked wrong. Never settle for a mistake.

How would you name your own paint range?

We recently created a collection with Irish paint company Fleetwood – the names are travel-based, including 'Rivington Rain' after a damp New York trip, 'Betsy' after a Miami hotel and 'Bofin Fern' after the Irish island.

Do you have a colour motto?

It's all about tonality and layering complementary tones, rather than having one strong colour.

Where do you visit for colour inspiration?

El Fenn Hotel in Marrakech is my number one – I remember walking in for the first time and I felt like I was stepping into a painting, all the colours and the materials … I could have cried. It opened my eyes to so much possibility.

Who are you following for interiors inspiration?

I love design brand Note Design Studio (@notedesignstudio), interior architecture firm Flack Studio (@flackstudio_) and design studio Sabine Marcelis (@sabine_marcelis). I have a million saved photos!

Top tips for decorating with colour

1. Start by defining the overall atmosphere that you want to create – colour and emotion are completely linked.

2. Map out the property, how you want to move through it, experience it and feel in each room.

3. Everyone has an intrinsic reaction to colour. Try and start to become aware of that, to look at different colours and see how you feel. Do you feel calm looking at forests or the sea, for example?

4. Always get paint samples! Even if it means delaying things.

5. Make physical mood boards and sample boards – ideally have a sample of every material that's going to be in the house and look at it in the room.

MARCANTE

TESTA

This Milanese apartment is formed around a memory. Created by Andrea Marcante and Adelaide Testa, the duo behind Italian architecture and design firm Marcante-Testa, the interiors of this inviting home reference the occupant's childhood throughout its colour and decorative choices. 'We asked her to think about somewhere she could remember where she felt calm and soothed, and she told us about weekend visits to her grandmother's country house when she was young,' explain the pair. 'It's a comforting memory in the middle of nature, so we introduced it into the project.'

Marcante-Testa's projects develop unique blends of colour relating holistically to the homeowner, the location, the building or its decorative details, and the story and palette are written from scratch. 'Traditions, culture and memories are all related to the emotional aspect of living, and we always try to find personal connections and inspirations within each project,' they explain. 'We use colour as one of our tools to tell the story of a space – it enables us to transmit messages and meaning, as well as create happy homes.'

Despite its central city location, the apartment is closely connected to nature through tree-level windows (through which the sound of birdsong is a regular feature) and proximity to a sprawling local park, which Marcante-Testa drew on for their 'grandmother's country home' aesthetic. Bucolic colours are spread throughout the space, creating a mood of story book escapism. The hallway becomes a richer green the further you venture along it, where you'll find rooms that may not have a garden view, but creatively conjure the rural. The corridor finishes in an all-encompassing emerald reminiscent of childhood drawings of trees, its vividness enticing you into the living area via an architectural room divider. A wall of leaves is ready to greet you, echoing the lush view of the windows either side of it and behold! Granny's within reach.

While the colour wheel was pointing firmly at green for the apartment's base palette, Marcante-Testa pushed boundaries in a quest to 'use colour in an unusual way', a mantra that often sees them challenge themselves to adopt tones that aren't found in their instinctive bucolic paint chart. 'Our approach is that if we dislike a colour we try to use it, because sometimes incorporating shades you wouldn't normally consider can help you explore a new path,' they explain. 'It's a way to find a positive colour attitude and explore new directions.' The salmon and mint bathroom is one success story resulting from this challenge – with the duo previously strongly averse to the pink hue – and it now adds an unexpected twist to the apartment, with images of the attention-grabbing room spreading like wildfire across Pinterest and Instagram thanks to its unconventional shades.

Previous page. The corridor culminates in a 360-degree painted flash of bold RAL '6032 Signal Green', drawing the eyes – and feet – along it and into the apartment. 'We wanted to create anticipation and suggest that perhaps you will discover something in the living room and dining room,' Marcante-Testa explain. The pair also removed the doors from their frames to flood the corridor with light and vitality.

Opposite. Quirky takes on nature fill the dining space and reference the outdoors. 'Colour is used as an architectural tool to separate two functional spaces, the kitchen and the table – the green resin floor defines the position of the table, a bit like a rug,' explain Marcante-Testa. 'Its colour reinforces the visual connection with the garden.'

A contemporary fable with a tongue-in-cheek twist, this fresh take on an old-school country cottage sees experimental shades and shapes toy with the traditional. Bold and calmer tones are delicately balanced, placed in just the right spot to draw you to the fresh air and leafy view, or to remind you of it. Greenness whimsically conjures leaves inside and out, a pattern of rainbow-tinted rain runs along the entrance hall, classic parquet contrasts slices of sage-coloured resin flooring, salmon leaps from the bathroom walls and a traditional floral carpet and pastel-toned fabrics add a spoonful of sugar to the living room.

Each zone in the apartment may have its own personality and role to play in the home's narrative, but the palette in every area is a carefully calculated balance of materials and tones, ensuring that when walking from space to space it all makes sense. 'Maintaining a continuity throughout the whole project is very important,' the designers explain. 'When you move from room to room, your memory maintains what you've seen before. So, when you are in a green room you register the colour, and the green remains in your mind and affects how you see the following space.'

'We never take ourselves too seriously – we believe that you can be thoughtful and playful at the same time,' say Marcante-Testa. 'For us, using colour is about contrast – sometimes we need calm shades and sometimes very strong, sometimes more joyful, sometimes subdued. It's always a mix, and a balancing act. Creating liveable, happy homes is our priority, and colour is a big part of that equation.'

Left. The multicoloured raindrops of the 'Showers' wallpaper by Maharam line the walls of the entrance hall, a hint at the indoor–outdoor theme of the apartment and its play on natural themes.

Opposite. Making the most of the apartment's wide corridors, Marcante-Testa turned the space into something functional, a one-wall library and reading area that merges retro mid-century shapes with contemporary furniture and lighting accents. The pale blue walls speak of bright Italian days.

The bespoke kitchen is divided in two, the upper half shrinking into the wall, creating the illusion of space and openness, the lower cupboards bold and eye-catching. 'Red is a difficult colour, which we only use in small amounts,' say Marcante-Testa. 'We love using it as an accent – these handles underline the kitchen.'

The open-plan living area is
surrounded by the enticing leaves
of Fornasetti at Cole & Son's
'Chiavi Segrete' wallpaper, with
each space divided by considered
architectural systems. A bespoke
cane-covered cupboard carves
out a living space, a cut-out resin
floor shape signifies the dining
area and the kitchen keeps out
of the way in subtle tones.

'The mood of the living room
is grandmotherly with a contemporary twist,' say the designers.
'We wanted a new carpet which
related to the past, and one of
our grandmothers had a traditional floral design like this – the pink
colours in it make the space more
playful and contrast with
the greens.'

Opposite. The contemporary rattan headboard from Maison du Monde references vintage metal beds while contrasting with a bona fide heirloom lace bedspread. The plant-covered 'Vårklockor' wallpaper by Josef Frank at Svenskt Tenn and the wardrobe-hiding soft-blue Kvadrat curtain create a mini landscape, framed, like a greenhouse, in a red metal grid.

Above. 'We wanted to bring back salmon pink from the 1980s to blend with the existing ceramicware's colour,' say Marcante-Testa. 'The bathroom is very much a colour experiment, simple but powerful.'

Do you have a favourite colour for the home?

Ressource Paints is our go-to brand as it has a wide range of colours that is divided by historic periods.

Are any hues banned from the house?

Probably fuchsia. It's difficult. Maybe that means we should use it in the next project!

Which space most benefits from colour?

Every room, every object.

Which colours do you like to combine?

At the moment, light colours with fluorescent shades.

Where do you visit for colour inspiration?

The Goetheanum, near Basel, combines colours on its stairs with concrete – it's really, really impressive.

Do you have a colour motto?

The same as Gio Ponti's: 'Everything in the world must be colourful.'

Have you had any decorating disasters?

Fortunately, not yet – we do a lot of testing.

How do you approach accessorising colourfully?

Play with fabrics, pillows, curtains and bedcovers.

Top tips for decorating with colour

1. Don't be afraid of colour.
2. Start with the shades already present in the building and expand from there.
3. Create mood boards with colours and materials.
4. Take into account natural and artificial light – test any colour on the walls and observe it throughout the day.
5. Remember bright, vivid colours really give us more energy.

CANDICE

LAKE

A colossal, gallery-like space comprising sky-high walls, organic shapes and constant daylight, owner fashion photographer Candice Lake's home was forged from a disused railway arch in Kennington, south London. After her husband Didier Ryan, architect and founder of Undercurrent Architects, had transformed the structure into a habitable house (the city's first residential arch), the space very gradually became an homage to all things bright.

With the entrance an unassuming doorway under an unassuming bridge, upon entering you're greeted by a dark hallway, an antechamber that readies the senses for the main event: venture through and you emerge, as if from a cramped Narnian wardrobe, into the unexpected – a three-storey burst of space and light sprinkled with dynamic pigment. 'It really is quite a magical thing,' grins Candice. 'I don't think I've ever had someone come in that hasn't said, "Wow!"'

Colour snuck up on Candice, tiptoeing into the home via the vibrant-yet-understated angular David Castro artwork she was given as a gift. Then it took on a life of its own, shoving aside her usual Scandi sensibilities. 'I didn't say "Let's make a multicoloured space here," – it just happened,' explains Candice. 'I started very, very gently, began adding and adding and adding and the colour just sort of grew.'

With interior-designer friend Pia Bayot Corlette nudging her along, Candice slowly developed a palette of primary tones in blocks or graphic formations that were drawn from the shades in the Castro painting. It was a gradual evolution, the home initially filled only by heavy dark-wood furniture and the art piece. Then came the rugs, the angular Rug Company design providing a soothing dash of pastel, then came the rest. 'My method was to bring in a bright chair and live with it to test it out and see how it felt – it was a discovery process. When I had the first pieces, I built around them, trying things and taking them out until it felt right,' says Candice. 'The house is bold, it's unapologetic and it's loud, but it's also very considered. I didn't choose anything just for the sake of having colour, I really focused on what was needed and really loved – the palette almost formed on its own.'

In the cave-like open-plan layout, rugs became room dividers, chopping the floor into manageable sections, each richly saturated. In keeping with the supersized scale of the building, colour is in sizeable chunks, the high-contrast primary scheme sculpted with hefty chairs, artwork and rugs, supported only by a minimal number of accessories. 'I like to bring in colour with big objects, as they create intensity and a sense of magic,' Candice says. 'I think trying to make changes with small knick-knacks is a big mistake.'

Blocks of brightness assemble in the living area, which is filled with a cacophony of expressive tones, materials and shapes. 'I like the juxtaposition here, how you're not really sure what's going on with the whiteness, the surprising shades and the mix of furniture – I don't like things to be obvious,' Candice explains.

Just as every piece was unhurriedly deliberated on, the textures too have come under scrutiny, with a wide range of materials and tactility giving the paint-by-numbers tones an authenticity and sophisticated feel. Then there are the walls. 'I really felt strongly about keeping the walls a blank canvas, and with that you have to make very brave colour choices,' Candice explains. 'I filled each area with colour using objects that that can be removed and changed – I don't think I would ever, ever touch the walls, as you need the neutrality to emphasise the brightness. Imagine how overwhelming it would be if they were painted.'

In a space that's at once cavernously vast and comfortingly cocooning, the colour – be it bottom-heavy – feels balanced, allowing the unusual architecture to sing and adding its own unexpected melody. Measured and deliberate, the high-impact, Crayola-set hues mean the interiors have a wildness to them, running riot across the lower level and bringing life, energy and dynamism to a home that could so easily be austere and overbearing. 'The reds, blues and yellows make the house feel so warm and welcoming, and when the day is a bit grey, they're utterly joyous and uplifting,' smiles Candice. 'Colour is exciting and a really brilliant way to bring happiness into your interiors – take risks and play with it, it's fun!'

Left. While used sparingly, colour defines this mostly colourless space, the zesty lemon armchair by Marc Thorpe at Moroso irresistibly drawing attention. 'We were just playing with the space, tried out the chair and now that's where it lives' explains Candice. 'I love experimenting with furniture.'

Opposite. Based around a bespoke table made from the top of a reclaimed school laboratory table, the dining area represents the simple style the duo started out with, and displays the painting by artist David Castro that provided the springboard for the home's palette. 'After we put the painting up, the colours from it spread into the house,' says Candice. 'It just sort of grew as we found pieces we were really drawn to, which happened to be in those tones.'

'The pale sofa pares things down,' explains Candice, with it offering an unexpected moment of whiteness that gives the vibrant armchairs, artwork, rug and cushions space to breathe. 'Its neutrality emphasises the other colours and draws your eyes down to the rug, which I think is the main attraction here.'

What's the best way to bring colour inside?

Buy pieces you love and the room will inadvertently come together. Know you will make mistakes – that's what eBay is for!

Which colours do you like to combine?

Yellow with pink and green – endlessly joyous and playful.

Are any hues banned from the house?

Anything purple is banished from my home – I have always had a deep aversion to it. I love to dress in orange, although I find it also a bit offensive in interiors.

Which space most benefits from colour?

If you want to experiment with textures, colours and prints, start in the guest loo! I love peeking into them when I'm at a friend's house as it is usually where you find the true spirit of the homeowner.

What's the easiest/cheapest/quickest way to add colour to a home?

A lick of bright paint is a quick and easy foray into a life filled with colour – it instantly transforms a room (and you can always paint it back!). Also, reupholstering a cheap second-hand sofa from eBay in a bright fun fabric is a wonderful way to experiment!

How do you approach accessorising colourfully?

Pull out three or four colours you love from large items in the room and build from there.

Have you had any decorating disasters?

If you don't love something, get rid of it. I bought a very ugly (but functional) flat-pack filing cabinet – every time I sat down to work it was glaring at me! Eventually I decided perhaps I didn't need a filing cabinet after all.

Do you have a colour motto?

Don't be afraid to be bold!

Top tips for decorating with colour

1. Don't be afraid to try things and make mistakes.
2. Start with a base item (rug or sofa) and build from there.
3. Experiment in a small space first.
4. Try to stick to three or four main colours.
5. Only surround yourself with things you love – if you do this, your home will always be filled with joy.

SELLA

CONCEPT

'When you think of colour, don't only think about primary colours – there are so many gorgeous, sensual shades that are incredibly subtle but which make a huge difference in the home,' says Tatjana von Stein, founder and creative director of interiors-and-design studio Sella Concept. 'Soft colours aren't just backdrops; they are atmosphere.'

Sella Concept has its fingers in a lot of design-led pies. Its sister brand Sella ID, run by Tatjana's wife and business partner Gayle Noonan, creates visuals and graphics, while Tatjana also has a furniture-design brand which melds Modernist sleekness with movement and dance. Lightly inspired by eras spanning the 1920s–1970s, the interior-design studio creates contemporary spaces mixing styles and aesthetics that are defined by senses other than sight. 'Our work is indulgent and welcoming, fluidly moving from totally calming to very sexy indeed,' says Tatjana. 'Sexy's where I want to be in terms of design.'

With Tatjana's background in set design, each of her projects is speckled with small moments of theatre that are like wry winks embedded in their chic surrounds. The performance starts as soon as you enter her apartment, with a yellow velvet-clad banister which almost purrs with plushness. 'I think it's kind of outrageous – it makes me smile,' she says. 'There's a theatrical sense of humour with it, I find the over-the-top-ness hilarious.' Then there are the small details that add flashes of colour, texture and shape, such as the abundance of floor-length curtains that remind us of an auditorium itself, and the set-like scenes created with curious objects at every turn.

The gold guest bedroom is rather little less subtle. It's not a gold-coloured, sunset shade. It's gold in a pirate's treasure chest, time-to-invest-in-gold, 24-carat way. The paint part of a set-design range, the incredibly rich, lush hue takes on the qualities of its nugget-y namesake, yet the startlingly lustrous walls are surprisingly grounding, calming and embracing. Aladdin's cave meets luxury hotel. 'It isn't as kitsch as it sounds,' explains Tatjana. 'I wanted to test it – and it's really beautiful, strangely, and so warm. It does make me smile.'

The apartment is widely presided over by 'Sella', a colour Tatjana and team created with paint brand Mylands specifically for her home (and now a permanent fixture in the company's paint chart), a kind-of-neutral with a yellow tint that has a mind of its own, changing dramatically depending on the room's light. Placed next to a more neutral tone on the hallway's back wall it becomes very yellow indeed, whereas in the living room it not quite but very nearly matches the bold yellow sofa and in the shadowy bedroom it's almost beige. 'It has an earthiness but it varies from a little bit pink to brown to yellow, it has

Plated head to toe in Mylands' 'FTT-001' paint, the gleaming metallic walls of the guest room are at the opposite end of the spectrum from the rest of the nature-inspired, creamy-hued home. 'I just wanted to play a little bit,' smiles Tatjana. 'Being in it is a lovely experience – unexpectedly really calming, and friends always tend to stay longer than expected ...'

a whole spectrum,' Tatjana says. 'It moves with the light and changes incredibly – overall, it's very sumptuous.'

The apartment's walls stick to three main shades, with the dancing 'Sella' neutral and the glorious gold and greens forming a backdrop for playful pops of colour and form. 'There's an elegance and a happiness that comes with these colours,' says Tatjana. 'They express part of me.' Comprising the top two floors of a classic Georgian home overlooking London's Hampstead Heath, it's no surprise that the verdant creeps into the apartment. 'It's nice to let the green on the outside come in – it adds another layer to the palette,' says Tatjana. The lush tones in the kitchen took inspiration from its original 1960s floor tiles, which feature a subtle spectrum of greens. 'People tend to try to make a small room bigger by painting it a pale shade, but I wanted to go for it,' says Tatjana. 'Working with different tones in the same family but in varied textures creates that indulgent feel.'

The apartment's ceilings are coloured in every room, yet you barely notice. Overhead hues come naturally, completing each space's scheme so unassumingly that once you've been engulfed by a room's colour scheme you can get on with surveying each space at ground level without distraction. 'I really love being in a womb-like environment and being fully immersed in a space, so I very rarely leave ceilings white – using all-over colour creates a full background so the room can focus on how everything moves together,' explains Tatjana. 'Non-white ceilings are a step away from the more traditional British houses, which usually have that very separated look – I think white just draws attention to the ceiling.'

'Colour is such an easy way of adding ambience to a space. At the moment my colours are calm, subdued and smooth,' says Tatjana. 'I don't tend be drawn towards the particularly bright, although that will probably evolve over the next six months. Once you start working with colour, it's quite hard to go back.'

Opposite. Walk into the home and you are immediately greeted by a is-that-what-I-think-it-is velvet banister in rich yellow that implores you to reach out and touch. The stairwell's walls painted in Mylands' 'Wharf Sacking' and 'Sella' introduce the earthy, golden glow that shines into every corner of the home.

A Fest Amsterdam sofa which out-brightens the walls presides over the living room, bringing brightness to the whole space and encouraging the 'Sella' paint to come over to the yellow side. 'The sofa brightens everything,' says Tatjana. 'It's about working with different tones in the same family but in different textures.'

Above. Engulfed in verdant hues inspired by the 1960s floor tiles as well as the apartment's leafy surrounds, the kitchen is painted in rich 'Bancha' by Farrow & Ball, accented by units painted in Mylands' 'Stockwell Green' as well as statement coordinating accessories. 'If you have a slightly non-room, why not make it into something interesting and indulgent?' asks Tatjana.

In the bedroom, Mylands' 'Sella' paint shows off its earthier side when hit by shadows and contrasted with glossy peach-coloured cupboards. 'The 'Sella' colour becomes muddier, which is really gorgeous and very, very gentle,' says Tatjana. 'It's calming from the minute you walk in.'

What's the best way to bring colour inside?

By creating a womb-like atmosphere with different tones and textures in the same colours.

Which colours do you like to combine?

Terracotta with any colour, because of its warmth.

Are any hues banned from the house?

I don't tend to lean towards blue in homes, unless it's a very dark shade.

Which space most benefits from colour?

Corridors – to bring them to life, as these are often dark corners of the house.

How do you approach accessorising colourfully?

Mix old and new and let accessories, table lamps and paintings do a lot of the talking. The more colourful the walls are, the more gorgeous colourful paintings look.

Have you had any decorating disasters?

Yes – when our bedroom turned into a glossy pink Barbie room accidentally. Sometimes you think you're ready for bold and you realise you want calm.

Do you have a colour motto?

I try to avoid rules – each room should have its own motto.

Where do you visit for colour inspiration?

My grandmother's flat in Paris, which sings with yellows and lime greens across silk walls, carpets and all-over patterns.

What are your colour goals for future projects?

I feel comfortable creating a world within a colour. The next step is to mix colours more.

Top tips for decorating with colour

1. Go for it.
2. Envelop a room with textures and shades of one colour.
3. Create worlds.
4. A lot can be done with accents, through accessories and painting.
5. Muted colours are still colours.

DANIEL

EMMA

For Daniel To and Emma Aiston, founders of product-design studio Daniel Emma, it's all about intuition. As designers of furniture, lighting and the occasional home accessory, their work is known for its simple forms and considered use of tones, each playful object generally coated in just one or two impactful hues. 'We often tie our colour choices or material combinations back to things that remind us of being kids – our work is childish,' they explain. 'We're inspired by simple everyday life, things such as food packaging with interesting graphics and shades. We aim to create objects that make everyday life a bit nicer, products that are in some way out of the ordinary, whether it's the shape or the colour.'

Their home in South Australia's Port Adelaide, an old worker's cottage built in 1910, is full of surprises, joy, charisma and generous dollops of colour. With a palette perhaps a little gentler than the brights they work with, the house is packed with fairly soft tones, interrupted by the odd pop of vividity. 'Because we use really bright colours in our own work, having our house as a slightly muted version of that gives us a little bit of respite,' the duo explain. 'If you have that intensity in a space rather than on an object, it can sometimes be a bit too much.'

There's no secret formula here, no hours of planning or careful deliberation – the decorative choices for this home were made instinctively, and almost alarmingly quickly, with an easy confidence that comes from years of working with colour. 'We go to the shades that feel intuitive to us, just because we like them and are drawn to them. There's no rhyme or reason – it's a bit haphazard and subconscious,' Daniel and Emma say. 'We chose the red for the big cupboard in one living room and the peachy pink for the bedroom wardrobes in about two minutes – because we've worked together for so long, making these decisions as a couple is very simple for us. The decorators checked with us about 50 times before they painted the red cupboards – they were more frightened than we were!'

The catalyst to the sunny yellow kitchen was a yellow Smeg oven, spotted in a store window and swiftly snapped up. 'The saddest thing is, the oven has all the bells and whistles in the world, but the only reason we bought it was because it was yellow!' Daniel and Emma say. 'We'll probably never understand its full capability ...' Once the oven was in place, the rest of the kitchen was shaped around it, with gentler coordinating lemon cabinets chosen after a whole week of deliberation – 'It was a big investment and we wanted exactly the right shade,' – and pastel accents (a blush-pink coffee machine, artwork by Alice Oehr and other small objects, as well as a built-in lilac alcove for the record player) add contrast. 'We were just drawn to those colours,' they explain. 'The way we collect stuff is very organic – it's just because we like it.'

Previous page. The main living area is where the most colour coexists in this house; different shades inhabit single spatial segments as showcased by the abstract artwork by Mignon Steele and the figurative Beci Orpin illustration. 'The pieces really complement each other,' say Daniel and Emma. 'It came together naturally – this room is more of a mesh of all of our collections.'

Opposite. A red-fronted cupboard brings a punch of brightness to the sitting room and contrasts with the 1950s fireplace. 'We chose the Taubmans' 'Paloma Sun' paint as we're not in the room often, it's a really nice surprise every time you go in,' Daniel and Emma explain. 'It's bright, but it's also calming, structured and controlled.'

There are some rules: Do. Not. Colour. The. Walls. Or the ceilings. Their bright whiteness emphasizes the light and air filling the space, lending it an art gallery-esque atmosphere. 'We would absolutely never use coloured paint or wallpaper, it doesn't even cross our minds – the idea of it feels really weird and claustrophobic,' say the pair. 'We would always have a white backdrop – white allows colour to speak for itself, and, without the contrast, it sometimes just doesn't work.'

This house is anything but austere, with lashings of rainbow-toned personality thrown at it. Colour is presented in chunks – on objects parcelled as individual pieces of pigment. 'We've always used block, segmented colour,' they say. 'We like that it's contained – it's like a painted wall is spilling out of its space. We like to keep colour in a controlled pocket. We design objects as individual components, and that carries through into our home. Colour is everywhere but it's not melding together or overlapping, it lives harmoniously but doesn't mix. It's got its place.'

'The objects in our home dance along the rainbow – it's a bit weird, and fun and happy. The combination of muted and high-contrast solid shades is interesting and it turns the house into a home, adding personality and making it feel like it's ours,' explain Daniel and Emma. 'Colour relates to everything, and an injection of it generally creates a happy or good mood. In Australia, there's not a strong history of colour in interiors – people are a bit frightened of it. But try something bolder if it feels right, it's worth the risk and it's not the end of the world if you get it wrong – it's fixable!'

Opposite. The yellow Smeg 'Portofino' oven led the way for the kitchen's brightness, the cabinets painted in Dulux 'Lemon Delicious' to bring in more sunshine. 'Yellow is a recurring theme for us. We're drawn to it because of the happy memories we associate with it, which is why we've ended up with so much' say Daniel and Emma.

The almost acid-orange pedestal supporting the table – a Daniel Emma design – adds another slice of interest and happiness.

A built-in nook is painted in Dulux's lilac-y 'Ace' colour, adding a bold yet subtle moment of contrast. 'We thought it would be a nice little pop of colour,' say the pair. 'It just felt good.'

Above left. A pink bath from the 1950s takes centre stage in the bathroom, complemented by coordinating powdery accents and a playful patterned curtain from Deny Designs.

Above right. Soothing block colours decorate the bedroom, a cornflower blue throw mixing things up a bit. 'The bedroom naturally evolved with subtler, more neutral colours,' say the couple.

The couple's working space is full of colour at every turn, with a painted yellow door interrupting the all-white backdrop. 'We amass objects in there in a much less structured way than in the house,' they say. 'It's a collection of samples, prototypes and Daniel Emma things.'

Do you have a favourite colour for the home?

Possibly yellow. It makes us happy.

What's the best way to bring colour inside?

Buying a colourful object! We own lots of bowls and vases – we always choose something practical and utilitarian that is colourful, rather than something like a sculpture.

Which colours do you like to combine?

A colour plus a natural material, like timber or marble.

Are any hues banned from the house?

No, everything has its place – in our house we have every colour.

What's the easiest/cheapest/ quickest way to add colour to a home?

Painting an internal door can make a big difference.

How do you approach accessorising colourfully?

Don't be afraid of colour and colour combinations – just feel confident and nine times out of ten it will work.

How would you name your own paint range?

We'd have food-related names, which is what we're drawn to when we select paint colours. Our yellow kitchen could be 'Paddle Pop Yellow' after the Banana Paddle Pop ice cream, which is exactly the same colour.

Do you have a colour motto?

No colour combination is wrong.

Where do you visit for colour inspiration?

When we went to Korea there were lots of normal, everyday spaces, like cafés and streets, with great colour and material combinations that were very enjoyable.

Who are you following for interiors inspiration?

We don't really use social media.

Top tips for decorating with colour

1. Take risks.
2. Have fun.
3. Don't worry about what your friends or family might think – pick something that makes you happy.
4. Travel, find inspiration in everyday scenes and draw from your own memories and experiences rather than following a trend.
5. Don't take it too seriously. People can get too caught up and stressed with the planning. It doesn't have to be as contrived as swatches and mood boards – it can be more intuitive. Relax!

A statement pastel gradient artwork by Evie Cahir brings balance to the home's bright, blocky shades. 'A big, bright, colourful picture would just be too much' explain Daniel and Emma.

STATE OF

KIN

Survey this three-storey concrete new build in Western Australia in one sweeping glance, and 'colourful' might not be the word that strikes you first. There's a lot to take in – decadent materials, natural patterns, minimalist principles and sculptural objects – but what ultimately gives the house its personality is the sprinkling of vividness used as a finishing touch to accent the building's arresting architectural splendour.

The structure and interiors are designed by Perth-based design studio State of Kin, the house is playful yet elegant, a dynamic melding of the flamboyant and the neutral, industrial and natural materials fraternising with generous splashes of brightness. 'We use soft tones as a support for the larger pieces so they don't take over the space, and then inject vibrancy with artwork and accessories,' explains Alessandra French, State of Kin's co-founder. 'We wanted the home to be a celebration of brilliant colour, rich texture, light and shadow – bold and expressive.'

At its core, the house focuses on materiality. It is lined with hand-crafted terrazzo floors, stained-oak parquetry, exposed-concrete ceilings and slabs of local stone – which is what makes its sudden chromatic switch all the more unpredictable and delightful. It could so easily have been a tonal sanctuary to all things found-in-nature, but not so. 'The unique timbers and stones provide a robust, rich foundation which is accentuated by flourishes of colour and curated playfully sophisticated furniture pieces and contemporary abstract art,' explains Alessandra. 'The timber and concrete elements that form the base of the palette create cohesion for the bursts of colour, graphic pattern, art and decorative fixtures. It feels really warm and welcoming, familiar and comfortable but still surprising and new.'

It's easy to envision this home without colour. It would look striking and elegant, both Instagrammable and timeless. But how would it feel? After seeing it resplendent in a full spectrum, imagining it stripped back to its albeit beautiful base just feels wrong and sad. This particularly bright palette, used so expressively, brings with it energy, soul and light-heartedness. 'Colour adds another element to a home. It evokes emotion and is such a vital part of design, igniting real joy,' says Alessandra.

With its multitude of organic components and jewel-like moments of colour, to maintain its clean, modern feel this building needs a breather, which is where the expanses of white come in. 'The walls provide a 'nothingness' that allows the heavier materials to have room, preventing the home from feeling closed in or too dark,' explains Alessandra. 'The white planes bring balance and harmony, allowing adjacent shades to breathe and create circulation around them.' There is one wow-factor exception to the

Previous page. The off-white of the sofa paired with the soft tone of the rug – both by Patricia Urquiola, at Moroso and CC-Tapis – and cushions creates interest without being overbearing, and is still calm. The pale sofa gives space for celebrating subtler colours and having fun with accent shades.

Left. Grey terrazzo, concrete and a minimal set of stairs are jazzed up with two imposing slices of brightness, an artwork by local artist Elle Campbell and designer Bethan Laura Wood's 'Super Fake' rug at CC-Tapis, an early indication that this house doesn't take itself too seriously. 'We wanted to create a feeling of joy, excitement, bright energy and vigour for the first impressions of the home – to inspire curiosity and hint at the layered, dynamic elements that will be discovered within,' says Alessandra.

non-painted surface rule – the simple yet spectacular bathroom, which combines terracotta-toned grout with a matching orange-hued sky. The ceiling is both wild and well thought through, a pumped-up version of the other earthy shades around the house. It's unexpected, like a guest you'd forgotten was coming to visit.

So, you've got your timber-floored, white-walled, marble-accented home. How to add in joyful colour without it looking like a clown has run amok? Firstly, make the most of the materials you already have. 'We played off the timber and concrete, softening them with warm, rich tones and lots of natural textures and pulling colour inspiration from the stones – chocolate brown, burgundy-plum red and terracotta all feature against a fresh white wall,' explains Alessandra. After you've eased in with drawn-from-nature hues, things get more powerful. 'We then layered in pastels and brighter shades with art and furniture to enliven the whole story, mixing in pops of teals, pinks and yellows.'

'It's refreshing to see so many designers around the world incorporating colour into their designs now – bringing refined but vibrant shades into your home can create energy and interest that will ensure you feel invigorated and vivacious. Life is too short to play it safe!' says Alessandra. 'There will always be a place for minimalism but bring on maximalism – designing with colour is so much fun!'

Left. The kitchen straddles the middle of the open-plan living space, creating a monochrome moment between two bright-tinged areas. 'We didn't want colour to compete with the exquisite granite island which is absolutely the hero in the kitchen,' says Alessandra. 'It has a strong, simple backdrop so it can really sing.'

Above. A statement artwork dominates the dining room, picking up on subtle colours within the space and introducing further brightness. 'We worked with artist Elle Campbell to create something vibrant and not too serious for the dining room,' explains Alessandra. 'She created a palette that complemented the fabrics and surrounding colours in the home.'

Next page. Hot 'Oriental Spice' paint from Dulux casts a permanent sunset over the bathroom, the colour coordinating with the bespoke shade of the grout, and Patricia Urquiola's Glas Italia's iridescent 'Shimmer' mirror acting as the sun and pulling in attention. 'When you see the mirror in different lights, it throws completely different colours onto the wall,' adds Alessandra.

What's the best way to bring colour inside?

Art – it brings another element to the space, it's always a talking point and can be moved or changed over time.

Are any hues banned from the house?

No, I think every colour has a time and a place.

Which space most benefits from colour?

Every room! Because why not?!

Where would you add a surprise hit of colour?

Bathroom ceilings!

Have you had any decorating disasters?

When I was 12 I begged my mum to let me paint my room lime green and pink … not my finest moment! I learned my lesson young, so no real disasters since then.

Do you have a colour motto?

Experiment, and, if you're not confident, hire a good designer!

Where do you visit for colour inspiration?

Local galleries – discover and invest in art! Support young and upcoming artists. There's a misconception that art has to be expensive but that's not necessarily true. Don't buy junk and don't buy into trends.

Top tips for decorating with colour

1. Be brave!

2. Before selecting a colour palette, really think about the way you want a space to feel.

3. Start with small injections of a single shade and build from there – if you're unsure, begin with a more neutral palette and layer colour in.

4. Try pairing different colours with a similar tone, or different shades of the same hue, but don't be scared to clash or layer colour and texture.

5. Do some research about colour theory and learn about hues/ tones/shades, etc – it's interesting and changes how you understand colour.

TRIFLE AND

FLOOR STORY

The East London Victorian home of Emma Morley, founder and creative director of commercial interior-design practice Trifle, and Simon Goff, owner of contemporary rug brand Floor Story, is one big adventure. Each room is its own island, filled with narrative and rich colour, floating unconnected to the space either side of it. At one turn, you're in a land of pink and striking black accents, then at the next you're standing on terracotta tiles soaked in sunlight.

'It's eclectic,' confirm the duo. 'There's a blend of contemporary and vintage tones, and the furniture's a mix of old and new. It's characterful, fun and energising'. Each room embraces you upon entry – welcoming snugs of spaces intent on convincing guests to stay a while, get comfy and look around. 'Each room is different in terms both of design and vibe, but it all flows,' Emma and Simon say. 'You're able to really transition from one very different space to another through the use of colour.' Colour reigns. Look up, down, sideways, behind you and there it is – a lot of it – giving each zone a distinct identity and imbuing the house with an almost palpable warmth.

'Our travels around the world have hugely influenced the look, feel, design and palette of our home,' say the pair. 'Some of it is more subconscious and subtle, and some more direct, but I don't think you'd walk into our house and think that the colours are classically 'British'. You can see that they come from other countries, and certain elements of Spanish and Moorish culture have definitely influenced our style.' The house's mustards, teals, oranges and pinks are indeed rich and intense, as if they've spent the day basking under a Mediterranean sun. Blues evoke a warm sea, flashes of yellow speak of the sun, peach points to baked clay, while the black floor downstairs makes every shade shine a little brighter. 'People say coming to our house feels like being on holiday, which we love,' the two smile.

If there's one thing that's universal throughout the space, it's the wow-factor, attention-grabbing, rule-defying rugs dotted in every room. 'For me, a room without a rug is not a complete room,' says Simon. 'They bring warmth and soul, and are a brilliant opportunity to gamble a little and lay down some personality with colour and design.' The rugs hold their own in this house, a mixture of bright and subtle, vintage and contemporary, shapely and squared, and daring and classic, all brought together like long-lost friends at a party. Setting the tone for the house, is 'Giovanni', the face-shaped rug designed by artist John Booth which greets guests as they enter from the hall; 'It shouldn't really fit there, but you go in and think, "Oh, that's a bit much, but it works,"' explains Simon. Covered in vivid, paint-like swooshes and heavy black lines, the rug could be a summation of the house

The living room is painted in 'Tropicalia' by Valspar, with the ceiling in 'Arabian Red' by Craig & Rose. 'I was a bit nervous when I first painted it,' admits Emma. 'I thought, "Oh my God, have I gone too far?" but we love it now.'

itself – unexpected, experimental, bright and cheerful ready to raise a smile.

During their 13-year tenure, the house has become increasingly vivid, the all-white walls slowly disappearing over time, never to be seen again. Chip away at the paint and you'd uncover gobstopper-like layers, the bold top colours becoming more and more subdued the deeper you go, a backwards timeline of the pair becoming more confident and turning the dial up on the shades they like. 'Year upon year we have added more colour until we've reached this extreme version of the house,' they explain. 'We do push ourselves to be brave with colour – why say it when you can sing it?'

In Emma and Simon's house, colour is a reminder of faraway places, their confident palette acting as a collection of soothing sun-kissed memories. 'Our colours have a very calming effect, which is really important to us as we're in such an urban environment. When we walk in from busy, bustling, stressful days, it makes us feel relaxed. It's our happy place,' they say. 'As much as we like to travel, we always love coming back home.'

Left. The modern stained-glass window in the door was designed by Emma. 'It introduces the colours that are in the house and gives you a little bit of insight into what you're going to get when you walk in,' she explains. The front door is painted in 'Sulking Room Pink' by Farrow & Ball.

Opposite. A 'Giovanni' rug by John Booth at Floor Story dominates the central space of the living area with its painterly splashes of bright hues. 'Some people ask "Why have you got a face on the floor?" It's crazy,' say the couple. 'The space feels calm then – bam! The rugs mix it all up.'

Opposite. The kitchen balances 'Pellezzano Mustard' tiles from Claybrook and the deep green Kent & London kitchen units (painted in 'Alpine View' by Dulux) on a warm terracotta tile by Solus in 'Trigon' Provenca finish earthstone. 'The kitchen was white, but now it's a buttermilk colour, which has added richness to it – it feels more like a colour you can eat,' says Emma.

'Arrange' tiles by Tom Pigeon form a unique interplay of colour and shape on the walls of the shower, picking up on the existing hues in the house.

Opposite. 'When we wake up, we see the rattan doors of the wardrobe so it's tranquil,' explains Emma. 'When you walk in, you see the ochre rug with the 'Tea with Florence' paint by Little Greene and it's all quite lively. It's a room of two halves.'

FAILE

What's the best way to bring colour inside?

Paint the walls! We're not very brand loyal – we love Little Greene, Valspar, Dulux, Farrow & Ball and Paint and Paper Library.

Are any hues banned from the house?

No, we are always open and there is a place for every colour; also, tastes change over time.

What's the easiest, cheapest, quickest way to add colour to a home?

With rugs, because you can be brave, go bold and have fun with them, and walls as they are the most cost-effective way to add colour.

Have you had any decorating disasters?

Yes, we tried ochre and pink in our hallway and it so did not work – one day we'll find a way to make them work because we know they can!

Do you have a colour motto?

Go with your instinct and what you love. Do not fear colour, have fun.

How would you name your own paint range?

A dream job! We would choose something humorous or musical with relevance to the colour: the living room should definitely be 'Club Tropicana' (it's 'Tropicalia' by Valspar).

Where do you visit for colour inspiration?

El Fenn in Marrakech, the Gubi flagship store in Copenhagen and the Alhambra in Granada. Also, Mexico and Colombia in general are filled with incredible colour combos.

Any colour goals/wishes for future projects?

To paint more ceilings! And to add more random pops of unexpected colour.

Top tips for decorating with colour ...

1. If you are nervous, pick an object that you love and design the décor around that.
2. Stick to three complementary colours/tones.
3. Don't panic if you hate it at first. Live with it for a while and see if you get used to it (sometimes a change is a shock!). You can always repaint it!
4. Go bold in a small room or toilet first.
5. Sample the hell out of stuff! Use tester pots to paint A4 sheets of paper, try them on different walls and make sure you look at them throughout the day in different lights.

The faded pink shades of the vintage rug from Floor Story coordinates with the pale pink wall painted in 'Pink Ground' by Farrow & Ball. 'We'd like to go bolder in there soon...' say Simon and Emma.

K&H

DESIGN

For Katie Glaister, founder of K&H Design, colour in the home comes down to research. 'We spend a huge amount of time with homeowners, teasing out what they are drawn to,' she explains. 'It's a very formal process – we ask them a lot of questions, such as what their favourite hotel is, or their favourite restaurant, or their favourite artist, so we can begin to visualise their style and start building colour palettes.'

Each of K&H Design's projects is strikingly different from the next, as unique as the people that commissioned them. One theme that binds them? 'It's the joy of colour, rather than a common palette,' says Katie. 'To us, colour is happiness. It's fun for your eye to be drawn from one room to another by colour, to create a journey with it.'

This West London Victorian home is quite the adventure for the eyes, its owners inviting the bold, bright, wacky and playful. Enter through a vivid yellow front door – a clue to what you might find beyond – and, straight away, the hallway says it all. A river of colourful floor tiles approaches a vivid stair runner, which sits above a wallpaper bedecked in pink and red leaves. It's a lot to unpick, but somehow – thanks to the encircling white walls – it doesn't overwhelm. 'Look up the stairs and you've got very fine panelling and calmness and light, so it allows it all to play very intensely just for a little moment,' explains Katie. 'Tonally, it's all singing together.'

The runner is a story in itself, a literal colour thread tying the home together, the bespoke 30-metre-long kilim-style weave decorated with chunks of hues found through the house. Cheerfully inviting all that stand at its starting point to wander its full length along and up the building, it succinctly sums up the surrounding shades. 'The runner celebrates and brings together all of the colours in the project,' says Katie. 'It takes the eye on a journey from room to room – what fun it is!'

Another constant is a zingy celadon, the tone present in almost every space, a smiling friend among the crowd of new shades and styles that gather behind each door. Starting in the hallway, outlining the initial explosion of brightness in ornate, aqua-framed glazing, the vivid celadon continues to pop up in big and small offerings, standing centre of attention on the kitchen island, lightly alluded to in the dining area via the chairs, storage and accessories, in the painted backdrop to the main bedroom and hiding among other colours in the family room. Notice it once, and it emerges at every turn. 'It's not a lot,' says Katie. 'But it just pulls it all together.'

There are other tones, a lot of them. 'For us, typically there are around 70 different colours in a project,' explains Katie. 'This one has something like 168 – it was mind-blowing as we put it all together.' Such a high hue count may be surprising for a house with so many white surfaces,

With so much action at ground level, almost everything from the feet up in the hallway was made calming, simple and colourless. The tones in the Victorian floor tiles by London Mosaic and sage green 'Persian Palm' wallpaper by Ottoline are just some of the colours in the house that contribute to the shades decorating the bespoke stair runner, all watched over by the decorative window frame painted in Little Greene's aqua 'Tabernacle'.

239

yet it's what goes on within them that gets the tally rising. 'Yes, the walls are white, the shutters are white and the ceiling is white,' Katie says. 'We put strong tones in the middle of the room, so they become glorious celebrations of colour, bold rather than distracting.' These dramatic shades congregate in the centre of rooms in blocks, a rich green sofa and red rug for the living room, the vivid kitchen island, a reading nook nestled into the wall of the family room, each space forming its own colourful vignette, supported by an expansive pale frame.

The scheme for this unique, joyful house initially revolved around pieces of art the owners had, the varied palette widening and gathering a life of its own through careful planning stages, concepts, communication, mood boards and testing. 'Interior design is so open now – there are just ideas everywhere,' says Katie. 'There's an abundance of colour and design at the tips of all our fingers. You can see how colour in the home works and it's exciting, creating the confidence to embrace it. It's like a sweetie jar – there's just so much out there.'

Opposite. The colour starting point in the family room was the Cole & Son's 'Savuti' wallpaper, which lends its tones to the bespoke lino floor from Sinclair Till, the Tolix seats and the cushions from Vanderhurd and Oka.

'It's confidently eclectic,' says Katie of the living room. 'It's delicate but it also has a huge playfulness.' A melange of colours meet in the middle of the room – the green velvet 'Roubel' sofa by Pinch, a vivid rug by Marguerite Le Maire, the pink 'Charlotte' chair by India Mahdavi, topped off by the vivid 'Origami Stripes' coffee table by Patricia Urquiola for Budri.

The kitchen is almost colourless save for the characterful island, its top made from Pyrolave volcanic lava in 'Vert Mousse' and painted in Little Greene's 'Pall Mall' to match the built-in pantry, creating a soothing statement at once bold and calm.

Opposite. Striking a different, calmer tone than the rest of the house, the main bedroom is coated in the soothing shades of Farrow & Ball's 'Green Blue' paint, supported by the whimsical, dream-like 'Oasis' wallpaper mural by Woodchip & Magnolia.

Above. Pastel-toned sanitaryware gives the children's bathroom a playful, story-book feel, the toilet in sky blue, cistern in primrose and the seat in coral pink, all from Broken Bog. 'It's crazy – we just thought "Why not?"' smiles Katie.

Do you have a favourite colour for the home?

'Celadon' by Argile. It invites so many other colour palettes to it, it's forgiving and adaptable with a warmth, yet has a brightness about it.

Which space most benefits from colour?

Every room can benefit from colour in any shape or form.

What's the easiest/cheapest/quickest way to add colour to a home?

Paint the walls, or paint a door. It changes the character of a room, it's quick to paint and easy to repaint if you don't like it.

How do you approach accessorising colourfully?

Plan your lighting. Lighting makes or breaks any scheme in any room. The placing of those lights just to hit on that colourful accessory will be sublime.

Have you had any decorating disasters?

Touch wood, not yet!

How would you name your own paint range?

After colours of the earth and the beautiful places on our planet. I would call this house's aqua tone 'Plitvice' after a very beautiful lake in Croatia.

Where do you visit for colour inspiration?

What I would like to do is go on tour of all of the Orthodox churches of Ethiopia and Greece and to take inspiration from the interiors – the interior murals and the ceiling decorations are intensely rich in colour and detail, and depictions of home scenes.

Who are you following for interiors inspiration?

Paint brand Edward Bulmer (@edwardbulmerpaint), craftsperson Margit Wittig (@margitwittig_artist) and painter Flora Roberts (@flora.roberts).

Top tips for decorating with colour

1. Find a place to start, such as with an object or a painting.
2. Think about flow.
3. Test paints! Don't rely on what it says on the tin.
4. Paint samples onto lining paper.
5. Look at the samples at different times of the day and night, and with the lights on and off.

The diminutive WC breaks the house's pale-wall rule, fully immersed as it is in high gloss '90GY 21/472' paint by Dulux Trade. 'It's bold, playful – just cool,' says Katie.

251

CREDITS

Every reasonable effort has been made to acknowledge the copyright of artworks, furniture and homewares in this volume. Any errors or omissions that may have occurred are inadvertent, and will be corrected in subsequent editions provided notification is sent in writing to the publisher.

STINE GOYA

Page 10
Art – Cathrine Raben Davidsen

Page 12
Art – personal collection of photographs, lithographs and souvenirs
Lights – Helle Mardahl Studio
Bench – Piet Hein Eek

Page 14
Art – John Kørner

Page 15
Sofa – bespoke
Art – Tal R

Pages 16–17
Art – Ulrik Weck
Sofa – vintage
Armchairs – vintage
Ceiling light – Fos
Floor lamp – Isamu Noguchi at Vitra

Page 18
Mirror/art – Lex Pott and David Derksen
Art in hallway and small piece – Casper Sejersen

Page 20
Art – Tal R
Chair – vintage Casper Sejersen at Carl Hansen & Søn
Pendant – Ana Kraš at Hay

Page 21 (left)
Art – Anne Torpe

Page 22
Wardrobe – Muller van Severn at Reform

EARL OF EAST

Page 24
Art – Atelier Cph at Earl of East
Sideboard – Habitat

Page 26
Art (right) – Studio Lenca
Art (left) – Jason Tessier
Sofa – Arlo & Jacob

Page 28
Wall hanging – vintage Japanese Noren

Page 29
Art – Hugh Holland
Bespoke table and stools – Fred Rigby
Daybed – Ilse Crawford at Ikea

Page 32
Framed photo print – Ana Kerin
Bed – Ikea
Chair – vintage

Page 33
Screen print – James Wilson
Bed – Ikea
Side table/stool – Soho Home

Page 34
Table – bespoke
Chair – vintage

REGAN BAKER

Page 36
Art at the top of the stairs – Tonya Thornton
Art above fireplace – Jenny Sharaf
Chair – Traba

Page 38
Light – Allied Maker
Table – Lawson Fenning
Sofa – EQ3
Rug – Atacama
Side chair – Traba
Pendant light – Trueing

Page 40
Stool – Tolix

Page 41
Art (left) – Kota Ezawa
Art (right) – Luz
Chairs – Division 12
Table – Sobu
Pendant light – Trueing

Pages 42–43
Art – Julie Blackmon

Page 44
Art above bed – Alexander Calder
Bedside cabinet – Frank Haller at USM
Chair by vanity area – Chairish
Bed – EQ3

EVA–MARIE WILKEN

Page 50
Art – Lone Seeberg
Table – Warren Platner at Knoll
Sofa – Fogia
Light – Greta M. Grossman at Gubi
Rug – Base 212

Page 52
Art – vintage
Chair – Fritz Hansen
Side table – Sebastian Herkner at Classicon
Ceiling lights – Jaime Hayon at &Tradition
Table – Warren Platner at Knoll
Sofa – Fogia

Page 54
Grey abstract art – Eva-Marie Wilken
Light – Cottex

Page 55
Art – artist unknown and antique
Rug – Boho-me
Lighting – flea markets
Chairs – Gastone Rinaldi
Tables – Woud

Page 57
Poster – Permild & Rosengreen

Page 60
Bench – Woud

CLAUDE CARTIER

Page 62
Runner – Patricia Urquiola at CC-Tapis

Page 64
Chair – Pierre Paulin at Gubi
Chandelier – Magic Circus Éditions

Page 66
Runner – Alix Waline at Pinton

Page 67
Bench – Big-Game at Moustache
Rugs – CC-Tapis

Page 69
Wall lights – Magic Circus Éditions
Sofa – Patricia Urquiola at Moroso
Pendant– Giopato & Coombes
Screen – Ronan & Erwan Bouroullec at Glas Italia
Rug – Patricia Urquiola at CC-Tapis

Page 70
Pendant – Flos
Sofa – Baxter
Rug – Faye Toogood at CC-Tapis

Page 71
Tables – Christophe Delcourt
Yellow chairs – Gebrueder Thonet Vienna
Light – Éric de Dormael at DCW Editions

Page 72
Rug – Elena Salmistraro at CC-Tapis
Headboard – Claude Cartier Décoration
Mirror – Jean-Baptiste Fastrez at Moustache
Armchair and bench – GamFratesi at Gebrueder Thonet Vienna

FLEUR DELESALLE

Page 76
Posters – Galerie Kasia Michalski
Orange sofa – Philippe Malouin at SCP
Mustard chair – vintage
White chair – Pierre Paulin at Gubi
Tables – bespoke Fleur Delesalle
Rug – bespoke Fleur Delesalle
Light – vintage Carlo Nason

Page 78
Mustard chairs – vintage
Green chair – Pierre Paulin at Ligne Roset
Sofa – Tacchini
Rug – bespoke Fleur Delesalle
Table – vintage
Gold light – Louis Weisdorf at Gubi

Page 80
Light – Lee Broom
Table – bespoke Fleur Delesalle
Bench – bespoke Fleur Delesalle
Chairs – Thonet
Kitchen island – bespoke Fleur Delesalle
Terrazzo – Max Lamb

Page 81
Art – Damir Ocko collage
Ceiling lights – Dechem Studio at Bomma
Chairs – Vincent Sheppard
Table – bespoke Fleur Delesalle
Light on sideboard – Giacomo Castiglioni at Flos

Page 82
Art – Jean-Charles Blais

Page 83
Bed – bespoke Fleur Delesalle

Amy Moorea Wong is an interior-design journalist who has written about all things home-related for over a decade, including as features editor at *ELLE Decoration* and news editor at *Livingetc* magazine. She is an ardent believer in the power of the home to ignite happiness and fiercely wants to spread the word that colours on surfaces, ceilings, shelves and sofas shouldn't be scary, but welcomed inside as important moments of pleasure. Her love for cleverly deployed primary colours plus pops of pink and natural materials (on which to rest the eye) in her home is something she is continually nurturing and experimenting with.

Published in 2023 by Hardie Grant Books,
an imprint of Hardie Grant Publishing

Hardie Grant Books (London)
5th & 6th Floors
52–54 Southwark Street
London SE1 1UN

Hardie Grant Books (Melbourne)
Building 1, 658 Church Street
Richmond, Victoria 3121
hardiegrantbooks.com

British Library Cataloguing-in-Publication Data.
A catalogue record for this book is
available from the British Library.

Kaleidoscope
ISBN: 978-1-78488-546-5

1 3 5 7 9 10 8 6 4 3 2

Publishing Director: Kajal Mistry
Acting Publishing Director: Emma Hopkin
Commissioning Editor: Eve Marleau
Senior Editor: Chelsea Edwards
Designer: Daniel New
Copyeditor: Gillian Haslam
Proofreader: Jessica Spencer
Senior Production Controller: Sabeena Atchia

Colour reproduction by p2d
Printed and bound in China by
Leo Paper Products Ltd